SHORT WALKS FROM
West Yorkshire Pubs

Leonard Markham

COUNTRYSIDE BOOKS
NEWBURY, BERKSHIRE

First Published 1996

COUNTRYSIDE BOOKS
3 Catherine Road
Newbury, Berkshire

ISBN 1 85306 442 4

Designed by Mon Mohan
Cover illustration by Colin Doggett
Photographs by the author
Maps by Ian Streets

Produced through MRM Associates Ltd., Reading
Typeset by Paragon Typesetters, Queensferry, Clwyd
Printed by Woolnough Bookbinding Ltd., Irthlingborough

Contents

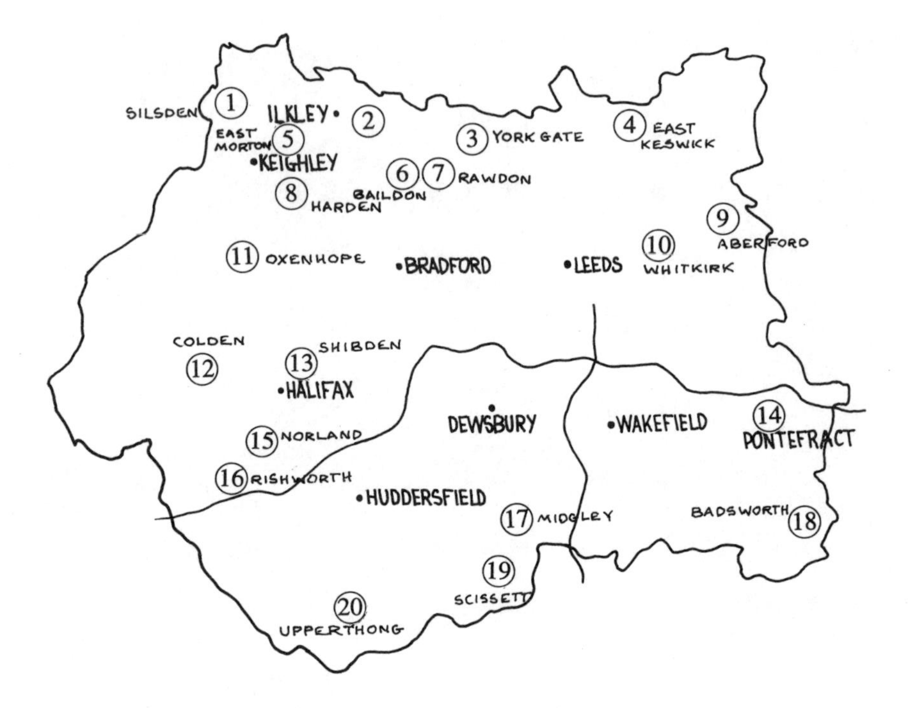

Area map showing locations of the walks.

Publisher's Note

We hope that you obtain considerable enjoyment from this book; great care has been taken in its preparation. However, changes of landlord and actual closures are sadly not uncommon. Likewise, although at the time of publication all routes followed public rights of way or permitted paths, diversion orders can be made and permissions withdrawn.

We cannot of course be held responsible for such diversion orders and any inaccuracies in the text which result from these or any other changes to the routes, nor any damage which might result from walkers trespassing on private property. However, we are anxious that all details covering the walks and the pubs are kept up to date and would therefore welcome information from readers which would be relevant to future editions.

Introduction

The county of West Yorkshire is triply blessed – superb countryside, an archaeological and industrial legacy second to none and some of the most inviting public houses in England. Pedestrian routes through the area are numerous, the longer and more rugged rambles having been well covered in my four companion volumes of *Pub Walks in Yorkshire*. I know from the popularity of those books that the combination of fresh air, attractive scenery, healthy exercise and encounters with pints and platters is a winner. And yet, on occasions, the longer walks, precluded perhaps by lack of time or fitness, are not always suitable for everyone – hence this book.

These mostly short and easy ambles over flat terrain are, with just one exception, recommended for all ages. Easily accomplished in a morning or afternoon and married with inviting pubs, many of which have facilities for children, the walks are particularly ideal for families.

Each of the walks is circular, and based on a selected pub. Along with the route descriptions I have included details of places of interest along the way. In the accompanying text I have also given information about nearby attractions and places of entertainment. All in all, here is a perfect compendium of delights for enjoyable days out in the West Yorkshire countryside.

A word on practicalities. It is always advisable to go equipped for the vagaries of the British weather. A good pair of boots, or strong shoes, and waterproofs, even in the height of summer (it's been known to rain!) are essential. And I would recommend the companionship of a good map, a hot Thermos of tea and a bar of chocolate. To elucidate further on the subject of maps; I have listed the OS Landranger sheet numbers with each walk but for the record here are the map titles as well – 103 Blackburn, Burnley and surrounding area, 104 Leeds, Bradford and Harrogate area, 105 York and surrounding area, 110 Sheffield and Huddersfield area, 111 Sheffield and Doncaster area.

As far as car parking is concerned, although landlords have

given prior permission for customers to leave their vehicles at these inns whilst out walking, I would suggest it is advisable to notify them first.

And now for the fray. Tighten the sinews, strain the laces and be off with you! And if you see me in the bar afterwards – it's your round.

Leonard Markham
Barwick-in-Elmet
Spring 1996

1 Silsden
The Punch Bowl

This gritty stone-built town of terraces, chimneys and factory yards was reputedly the last Yorkshire stronghold against the legions of Rome. Nail making and clog manufacture were once important and the Royal Navy's demand for sails during the 18th and 19th centuries spurred the development of linen mills, some of which now produce synthetic fibres. Of great interest are the old terraced rows close to the town centre. A colourful narrow boat marina on the Leeds and Liverpool canal is an attractive local feature. Above the town is the arcane and extensive Rombolds Moor with its strange Druidical circles, cairns and standing stones.

Often northern buildings wear their antiquity like frowns, the sooty patina of centuries hiding the warmth of virgin stone. The solution? Water and blasted sand! The success of such cleansing operations is nowhere more striking than here, where the Punch Bowl beams out from the bland, the attractiveness of its honeyed façade further enhanced in summertime by hanging baskets and a foil of border plants. There is an extremely pleasant front seating area among the flowers. Dating from 1784, the much altered inn has expanded into adjacent cottages over the years. Today it offers the very best in modern facilities, its immaculately presented interior furnished in velvet tones, the accent, heightened by a gallery of romantic pictures, being on comfort and relaxation.

The popularity of the Punch Bowl with locals says much about its value and service. The simple standard menu, consisting of sandwiches, jacket potatoes, chicken, chilli, jumbo sausage and haddock is supplemented by a daily-changing main dish, typical examples being prawn and haddock bake, quiche lorraine and gammon and eggs. A low-priced Sunday lunch attracts a large following – come early! Children have their own menu and senior citizen 'specials' are served on Wednesdays. Bar-top, the line up is hand-pulled Tetley, Boddingtons and Bentley's Bitter, Boddingtons Mild, Heineken and Stella Artois lagers and Guinness and Murphy's stouts.

The opening times on Monday to Thursday are from

Silsden Marina.

11.30 am to 3 pm and 7 pm to 11 pm, on Friday and Saturday from 11.30 am to 4 pm and 7 pm to 11 pm and on Sunday from 12 noon to 3 pm and 7 pm to 10.30 pm.

Telephone: 01535 652360.

How to get there: Silsden is easily reached along the A6034, either from Addingham in the north or from Keighley and Steeton in the south. The inn can be found in the centre of town near the town hall and police station.

Parking: The inn has its own car park. Overspill spaces (Silsden gets busy) can be found on local side roads.

Length of the walk: 3½ miles. OS map: Landranger 104 (inn GR 042466).

Along little-used, grassy tracks and quiet lanes within a few minutes' walk of Silsden's crowded streets, the route visits meadows and dells with long distant views to the south and east. There are several fascinating farmhouses along the way.

The Walk

Turn left from the inn and go left on Bell Square, continuing straight ahead across the junction, along Hillcrest Avenue. Keep going forward on Back Lane and pass to the side of the Cobbydale Park housing estate on a track. Cobbydale is an old name for Silsden. Theory one links the name with the local river; theory two with a Saxon term for fierce (don't ask the landlord to borrow a fiver!); and theory three with a Craven word for spiders' webs, which were once said to be abundant in Silsden's houses.

At the griddle over the beck, keep right along the beck bottom and go right through a gap by a gate along a meadow bottom. Go through a gap by a gate and keep alongside the overgrown hedgeline, swinging right across a meadow to the edge of a conifer wood. Go left along the edge of the wood on an arc, to a stile by a gate. Cross and walk on between a wall and a fence, then steer left, heading for the top corner of a hedgeline by an old gateway. Go through, keeping straight ahead and heading for a gate to the left of Hay Hills Farm.

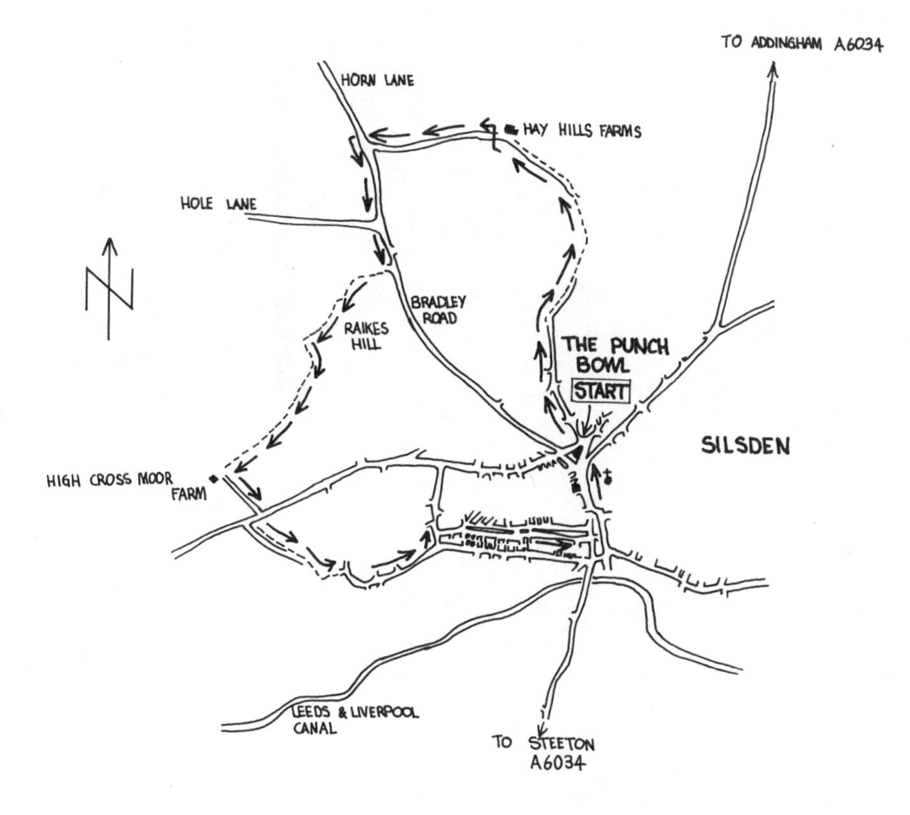

Turn right, following the yellow arrow-head marker, then take the access track off left and turn left along the quiet Horn Lane. Continue along Bradley Road and, 250 yards after the junction, turn right, following the footpath sign along the Bracken Hill farm access. Pass the farmhouse and go to the left through the farmyard, swinging sharp right on a descending track. Go left over the bridge and, at the top of the rise, keep going forward hedgeside and pass through a gap in the wall. Steer left for a gate across a meadow and cross a stile, going left, away from High Cross Moor Farm.

Continue to the road and turn right, then go left after 30 yards, following a public footpath sign. Go through a gate, keep fenceside and cross a stile in the field corner, following a yellow arrow marker across a field. Cross a stile by a gate and go left immediately through a gap in the hedge, steering diagonally left across an overgrown field, downhill towards the canal. Aim for a white post at the bottom edge of the housing development and go left along the narrow path, swinging left to Woodside Road. Turn right on Elliott Street and go left on Hawthorne Street. Turn right on South View Terrace and continue down Aire View. Turn left along Kirkgate and go left again, back to the inn.

Places of interest nearby
The wild expanse of *Rombalds Moor* lies north and east. Narrow boats may be hired on the Leeds and Liverpool Canal.

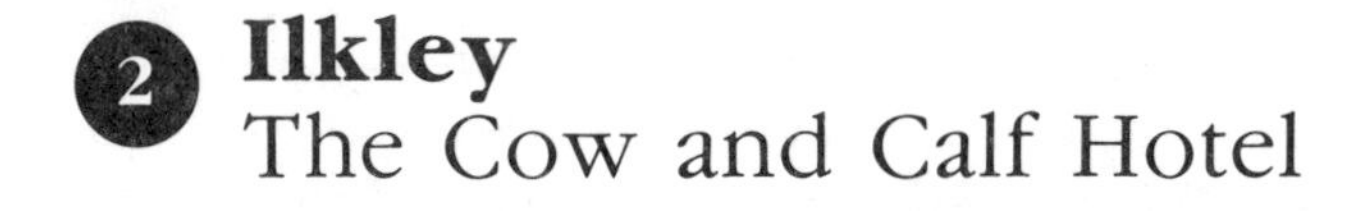

2 Ilkley
The Cow and Calf Hotel

Ilkley Moor, the home of grouse and the haunting curlew, is a mystical wilderness. The timeless human impulse to commune with ethereal forces is here writ large in strangely inscribed stones – scores of them – some dating from the Bronze Age. In complete contrast, the moor is the subject of a Yorkshire anthem. You may remember a snatch . . .

'The wurrms'll coom an' ate thee oop,
On Ilkla Moor baht 'at,
The wurrms'll coom an' ate thee oop,
The wurrms'll coom an' ate thee oop.

On Ilkla Moor baht 'at,
On Ilkla Moor baht 'at,
On Ilkla Moor baht 'at.'

Taking its name from a group of enigmatic rocks close by,

the splendidly positioned Cow and Calf Hotel commands panoramic views from the edge of this famous moorland. A former coaching inn, now offering luxurious 18-bedroomed accommodation and sophisticated food, the hotel has facilities for the many walkers who visit Ilkley Moor for the bracing airs and tangs of heather.

Most diners use the light and airy Jardin Room alongside the main bar. Dressed in leafy greens and furnished with garden-style furniture it offers open sandwiches – slices of the hot roast joint of the day served in a French stick are especially popular – snacks such as chicken and mushroom pancakes or more substantial dishes like grilled halibut, langouste à l'américaine and lamb cutlets. For more formal dining, customers can opt for the experience of the well-named Panorama Restaurant, an attractive venue for Sunday lunch. Authoritative trenchermen speak highly of the hot treacle tart and custard. Children are welcome here for meals. The house ales are John Smith's and Webster's Yorkshire Bitter. Carlsberg and Holsten lagers and Guinness are also on offer. The hotel has a small outside seating area for the warmer months and an award-winning garden (generally restricted for residents' use only, but open to the public on selected days during the summer).

The opening hours are from 11 am to 3 pm and 5.30 pm to 10.30 pm on Monday to Saturday. Sunday opening is from 12 noon to 3 pm and 7 pm to 10.30 pm.

Telephone: 01943 607335.

How to get there: The hotel is on Hangingstone Road, south of Ben Rhydding near Ilkley. It is easily accessed from Burley in Wharfedale, off the A65.

Parking: The hotel has its own car park, and there are other parking areas nearby.

Length of the walk: 2 miles. OS map: Landranger 104 (inn GR 134466).

These heathery heights are windswept and rock strewn and are not suitable for very young or aged walkers. But the views, the wild vitality of the moor

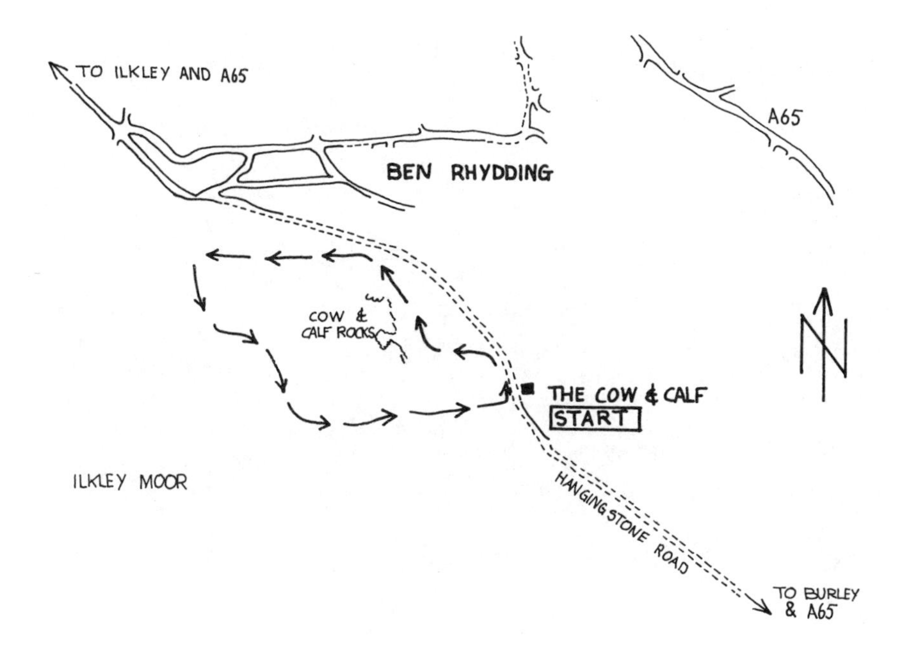

and the blooming August heather are better than any tonic – and the 'cup and ring' motifs and the ancient earthworks, circles and barrows are endlessly fascinating.

The Walk

Cross the road from the hotel, veering right, and walk towards the outcrop on the track running parallel with the road. Go left across the parking area up the stepped ascent. (The canyon in front, formed by old quarrying, is an attraction for novice climbers.) Steer right between the Cow and the Calf – readily apparent – and swing left on a very rough track, ascending and keeping to the top of the line of pine trees.

Keep going forward and, where the line of pines ends, turn left, heading for the narrow nick in the hillside, following the valley of the stream up left, with a waterfall on the right. Veer away left from the beck on a meandering path through bilberry and heather and, after about 100 yards, bear right on a green path, swinging left along a more substantial track towards a

Ilkley Moor from the top.

large boulder (see the incised symbols on its surface). Fork right and swing sharp left, following a rocky track downhill, back to the hotel.

Places of interest nearby
There are dozens of more extended walks across the moor (but remember that it can become featureless in bad weather – so beware getting lost).

3 York Gate
The Royalty

In a premier position above the high moorland of Otley Chevin, this ridge-top inn has served footloose visitors for many years. A modernised alehouse, its main attractions are a characterful tile-floored taproom, complete with a wood-burning stove, and a large family room. There is also a small lounge displaying pictures of local views. The long history of the inn is the subject of a framed text, hung alongside the 'most talked about cap in Clay Pigeondom'.

Sandwiches and bar meals are available lunchtimes and on Thursday, Friday and Saturday evenings, Friday night offering 'specials' in addition. The standard menu includes fried haddock and giant Yorkshire puddings, and traditional ham and eggs is a very popular dish. Children are separately catered for and have their own bar (at weekends) in the family room. A

A brisk climb on the walk near Otley Chevin.

Tetley house, the Royalty serves hand-pulled Bitter and Mild and Theakston Bitter. Lager drinkers can choose from Skol, Castlemaine and Carlsberg Export. The taproom offers entertainment on the piano from time to time and pub games (darts and board skittles). Outside is a patio/play area.

The opening times on Monday to Saturday are from 11.30 am to 11 pm (closed in the late afternoon in winter). Sunday hours are from 12 noon to 10.30 pm.

Telephone: 01943 2461156.

How to get there: The inn is on the roadside high above, and south of, Otley. It is best accessed from the A658 Pool to Yeadon road.

Parking: A large car park available at the inn. Additional free parking may be had 100 yards to the west, at Beacon House car park.

Length of the walk: 2 miles (plus an extra 1½ mile option into Otley). OS map: Landranger 104 (inn GR 206440).

This classic introductory walk over the famous Otley Chevin, now a designated nature reserve, traverses part of the bilberry clad moor. Breathtaking views encompass at least half of Yorkshire's landmarks. Short but immensely steep, the descent leads to the famous White House and on (if you wish) into the busy market town of Otley.

The Walk

Turn left from the inn along the road for 100 yards and bear right over the Beacon House car park. Go through a gap in the wall and walk on for a few yards to enjoy the 'surprise view'. Turn left along a track and stop by the toposcope (kindly installed by the Rotary Club of Otley). How many features of the landscape can you see? Holme Moss 26 miles, Great Whernside 22 miles, Brimham Rocks 13 miles, White Horse of Kilburn 30 miles, Almscliff Crag 5 miles.

Continue along the track. Swing right and then go left along a track on the brow of the ridge. Take the right-hand fork dropping downhill. After 250 yards, swing sharp right along a woodland edge track and gradually descend, passing the line of upright stones.

Turn left down the steps through the woodland and, after about 250 yards, go left to the White House tearoom and visitor centre. The tearoom offers light snacks in the summer months and is open from June to August inclusive, at weekends only – Saturday between 1 pm and 5 pm, Sunday between 11 am and 5 pm. The visitor centre exhibits wildlife tableaux and a farmhouse reconstruction and is open on Saturday and Sunday

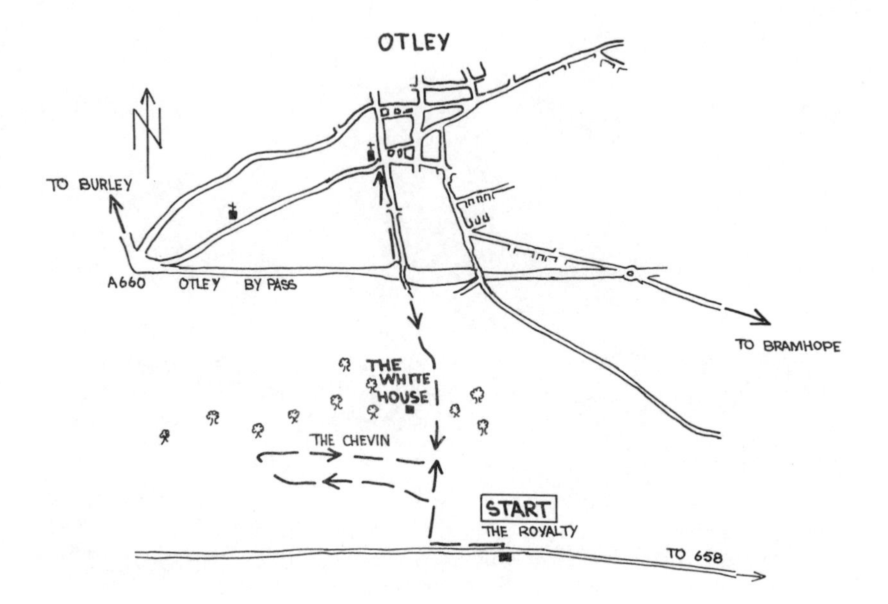

between 1 pm and 4.30 pm from April to October, and on Sunday only between 1 pm and 4 pm during November and December.

At this point, a very pleasant extension to the walk can be made by continuing down the hill into Otley. The route is well defined, having been originally constructed for Victorian visitors. The Cobblestones tearoom opposite the church is recommended.

To complete the walk, retrace the route upward from the White House, continuing beyond the steps along the right-hand footpath to the summit. Go through the gap in the wall onto the car park and make your way back to the inn.

Places of interest nearby

Spoking out from the Royalty, an extensive network of tracks beckon. Extended walks along well-defined footpaths can be made to Otley and Yeadon.

4 East Keswick
The Duke of Wellington

Apart from the regimental silver, this immensely comfortable country inn, situated in the pretty village of East Keswick, south-west of Wetherby, has all the accoutrements of an officers' mess. Decorated with famous battle scenes remembering the duke's finest hours, the spacious dining room and lounge, warmed by open fires in winter, offers relaxed eating and a robust menu. Home-made pies, such as beef and ale, steak and kidney and chicken, ham and leek, are a speciality. Attendant grills, roasts and 'Schoolday Puddings' – treacle roly poly and spotted dick – are the stuff that beat the French! Vegetarian dishes and children's portions are also available. The inn has a well appointed taproom, a small pool room and a patio area for the summer months. Hand-pulled Tetley Bitter is on tap, alongside Beamish stout, three lagers – Kronenbourg, Miller and Foster's – various ciders and a good selection of wine. The opening times are Monday to Friday

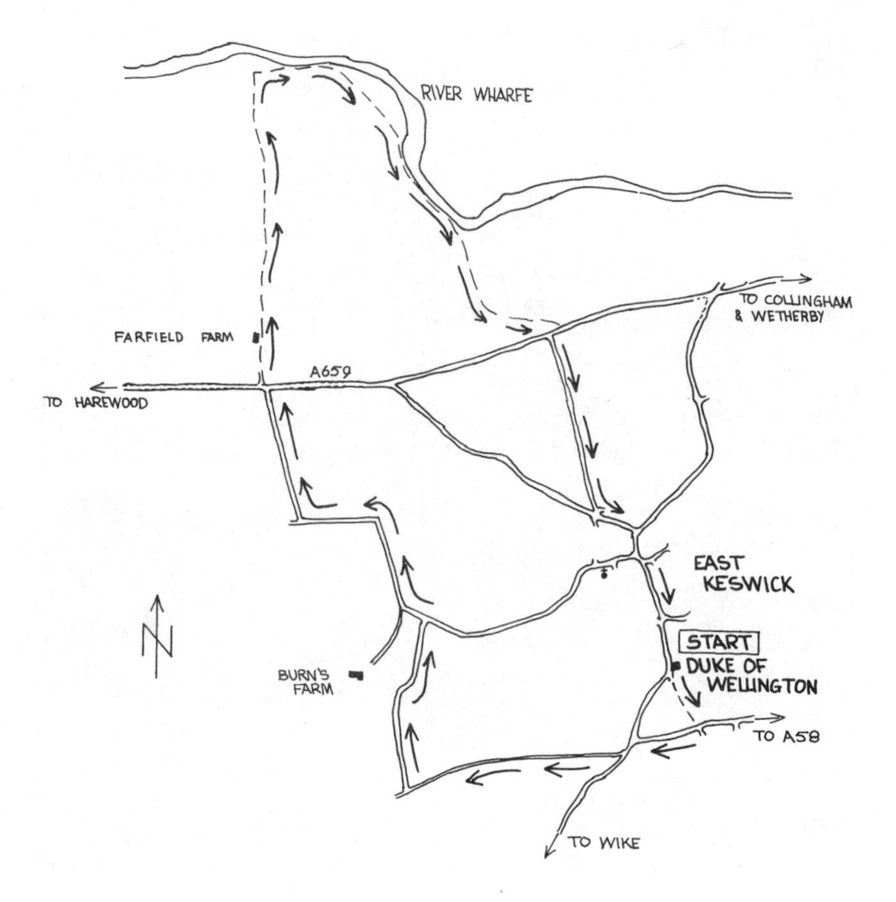

12 noon to 2.30 pm and 5 pm to 11 pm. Saturday opening is 11 am to 11 pm; Sunday 11 am to 10.30 pm.

Telephone: 01937 573259.

How to get there: The inn is in the village of East Keswick, west of the A58 Leeds to Wetherby road.

Parking: A large car park is available.

Length of the walk: 4 miles. OS map: Landranger 104 (inn GR 362443).

With panoramas spanning 60 miles, this exhilarating walk gives views hardly bettered by British Airways. Country tracks (be prepared for mud sometimes), bluebelled margins in spring, and a terrific prospect of the Wharfe valley, with long distant views of Almscliff Crag and the White Horse of Kilburn, combine in an energetic circuit that also explores attractive East Keswick.

The Walk

Turn left from the inn and go left by a quaint, castellated cottage, following the signposted public footpath over the Keswick Beck. Continue to a kissing-gate. Go through and cross over Keswick Lane to the footway. Turn right to the junction. Turn left, following the signposted road to 'Wike and Leeds' for 40 yards and go right along a marked bridleway. Continue for about ½ mile and 200 yards before the farm (near the white bungalow) go right, dropping down on a wooded track. Cross a beck and swing right to the road.

Turn left along the quiet lane and swing right around the bend, opposite the entrance to Burn's Farm. Walk on uphill and swing left and right along Moor Lane to the A659. Caution – high speed traffic, so cross with care. Take the signposted public bridleway to 'Farfield Farm', almost opposite. Walk along the gravelled drive, keeping straight forward between the converted farm buildings to a gate and a blue arrow marker.

Here a vista unfolds west and east. Such beauty inspired that famous Yorkshire foot-slogger Alfred J. Brown to write his lovely poem beginning 'There must be dales in Paradise'. Go through the gate, dropping smartly downhill, hedgeside. Cross a stile to the right of a gate and keep forward at the direction post, going over the field to the river Wharfe.

Turn right along the waterside path, the Ebor Way, swinging right by the hedge line. Cross a ditch (no bridge) and follow the direction post, keeping hedgeside. Swing right at the next direction post, away from the river (it can be muddy here after heavy rain) and go left, following the yellow arrow marker up to a stile. Cross and head uphill, bisecting the field. Cross a second and then a third field, veering left into the corner, and swing left along a hedge and ditch line to a stile. Cross onto the A659.

Go right along the verge for 50 yards and turn left down the

The Wharfe valley.

quiet lane. Continue to the junction and turn left into East Keswick. At the next junction, turn right along Whitegate and pass the Old Star, continuing back to the inn, where after such thirsty work this snippet from Brown springs to mind:

> 'There must be inns in Paradise
> Where nappy ale is sold,
> And beef and pickles – even pies
> Such as we've known of old!
> And we will find a parlour there,
> And call for pints for all to share!'

Places of interest nearby

Harewood House, west of the A61 – 18th-century stately home, with a tropical bird garden and an adventure playground for youngsters.

5 East Morton
The Busfeild Arms

East Morton, south of Ilkley and Rombalds Moor, is an attractive former mill village, its dapper cottages snaking the hills above the old beck sides. Of some antiquity, the Busfeild Arms, at the foot of a tortuous ascent, has expanded over the years, offering cosy public and lounge bars decorated with photographs of the working mills and local beauty spots. This one-time schoolhouse is noted for good wholesome food and CAMRA recommended ale.

Snacks such as toasted sandwiches and beefier choices like giant Yorkshire puddings, Cumberland sausage, home-made steak and kidney pie and gammon and eggs – followed by sticky toffee pudding – dominate the largely traditional menu although vegetable alternatives are available. Children are welcome at lunchtimes. The hand-drawn ales are Bass Light, Worthington BB, Draught Bass, Stones Bitter and Caffrey's. In a supporting role are Carling lager and Guinness. The inn has facilities for pool and a pleasant beer garden to the front.

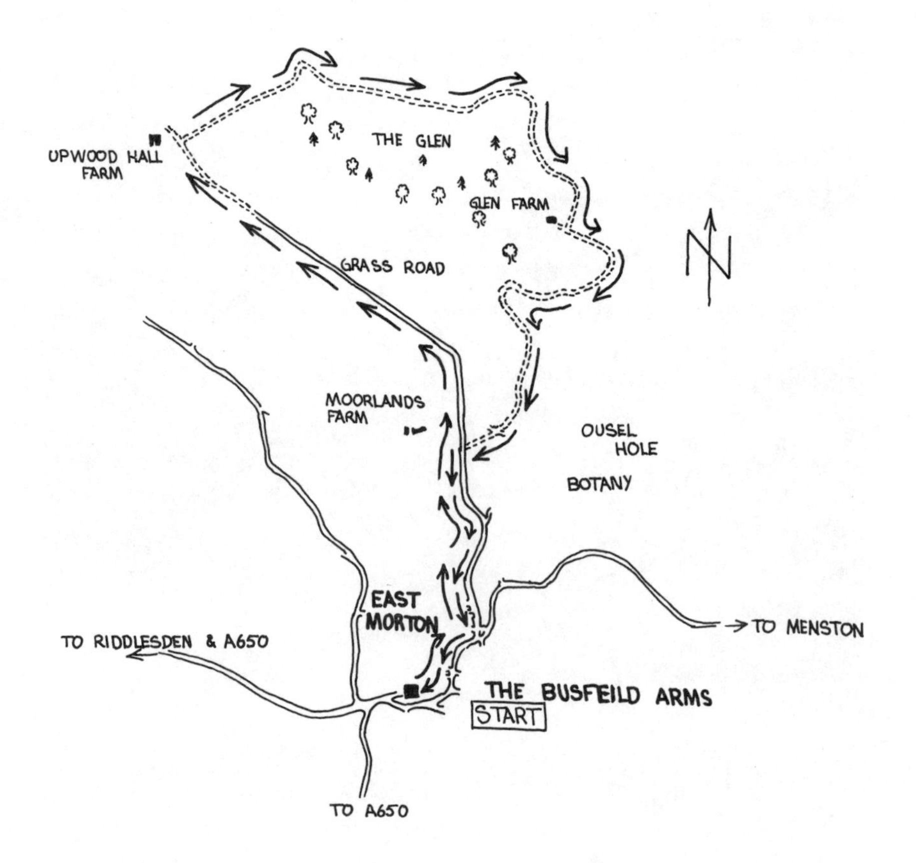

The opening times are from 11 am to 11 pm Monday to Saturday. Sunday hours are from 12 noon to 3 pm and 7 pm to 10.30 pm.

Telephone: 01274 564453.

How to get there: The inn is in the village of East Morton, to the north-east of Keighley. Approach from the A650 or take the more leisurely road from Menston or Guiseley.

Parking: Ample parking is available at the inn.

Length of the walk: 3½ miles. OS map: Landranger 104 (inn GR 099419).

Our outward route takes us by the village cottages, many lovingly preserved, right down to the painted mud scrapers by the front doors. The becks oozing off Rombalds Moor, to the north, provided motive power for the local mills and on this mainly moorlands walk you will discover, assimilated into the landscape, dams, conduits and mill ponds. Little used, the paths and trackways afford peace and solitude punctuated only by bleats and the cries of peewits. The route is hillocky in places.

The Walk

Turn left from the inn, along North View Terrace and ascend the hill, swinging right. Turn left again on Green End Road and pass the Methodist chapel of 1846 and its little cemetery. Go

East Riddlesden Hall. (Courtesy of Bradford Economic Development Unit).

Cliffe Castle Museum, Keighley.
(Courtesy of Bradford Economic Development Unit)

left, uphill, along Upwood Lane. Continue straight forward at the Moorlands Farm access, leaving the track and continuing along a stone-flagged causeway and then a green track bounded by dry-stone walls. Follow the dog-leg left and walk on, negotiating three gates and continuing towards the trees, then going through a fourth gate in the direction of Upwood Hall Farm, keeping the wall to the left. Continue towards the barn and go through the gap by the gate, immediately turning right along a track, heading to the moors.

Cross the beck and swing right, uphill, to a gate. Go through, following the yellow arrow marker towards a clump of trees. Continue through the next gate, keeping the wall to the left, and negotiate a third gate, swinging left and right to a fourth gate. Once through this, swing sharp right towards the fold building, go through another gate and steer left in front of Glen Farm. Swing right through the next two gateways and go left by the side of the farm, along the access road.

Following the arcing road right, downhill, cross the cattle grid and drop down in woodland towards the dam bottom. Swing left over the outfall, uphill to a kissing-gate. Go through and swing right to a second kissing-gate. Go through and turn left on Upwood Lane, making your way back to the inn.

Places of interest nearby

Within a few minutes' drive of East Morton a number of attractions give the option of 'making a day of it'. *East Riddlesden Hall*, to the west, is an early 17th-century furnished manor house owned by the National Trust. The grounds include a huge tithe barn, regarded as being one of the finest in the North of England. To the south in Keighley, are *Cliffe Castle* (a museum of geological history and folk life, with gardens that include aviaries, conservatories and play areas) and the *Worth Valley Railway* (steam trains).

6 Baildon
The Old Glen House

Perched high on its hill, precipitous Baildon commands long distance views of the Shipley, Bradford and Guiseley districts. The village was formerly known for its manufacture of worsteds. The principal local attraction is Baildon Moor, a lonesome wilderness haunted by curlews and exposed rocks marked with examples of Bronze Age art. Barrow excavations hereabouts have revealed cinerary urns, flint tools and daggers.

In a sequestered nook at the Shipley Glen summit, the Old Glen House, a former coaching inn, is remembered by many old time visitors as a tea room. Having reverted to licensed premises in recent years, it enjoys a premier position, being as synonymous with a trip to this famous beauty spot as the nearby Glen Tramway. Stone-built, revealing ancient beams and a cavernous fireplace, it offers a multi-level bar – diners get elevated status – and a public bar cum games room. Attached is a thoroughly modern and well-equipped children's play area with seating facilities.

Sandwiches and snacks are available, together with more substantial specials such as chicken in wine, cauliflower and broccoli bake, giant Yorkshire puddings and prawn brochettes. Children and the figure conscious (see 'slimmer's world' list) have their own menus. Barbecues are organised in summer, and live entertainment is always a feature of Saturday nights. Hand-pulled Tetley Bitter and Boddingtons and guest beers lead the bar-top line up. The alternatives are Skol, Lowenbrau and Castlemaine lagers and draught Guinness. Alongside the pub is a separately operated café.

The pub's opening times on Monday to Saturday are from 12 noon to 3 pm and 7 pm to 11 pm. Sunday hours are from 12 noon to 3 pm and 7 pm to 10.30 pm.

Telephone: 01274 589325.

The narrow boat water bus service can carry up to 46 passengers.
(Courtesy of Apollo Canal Cruises)

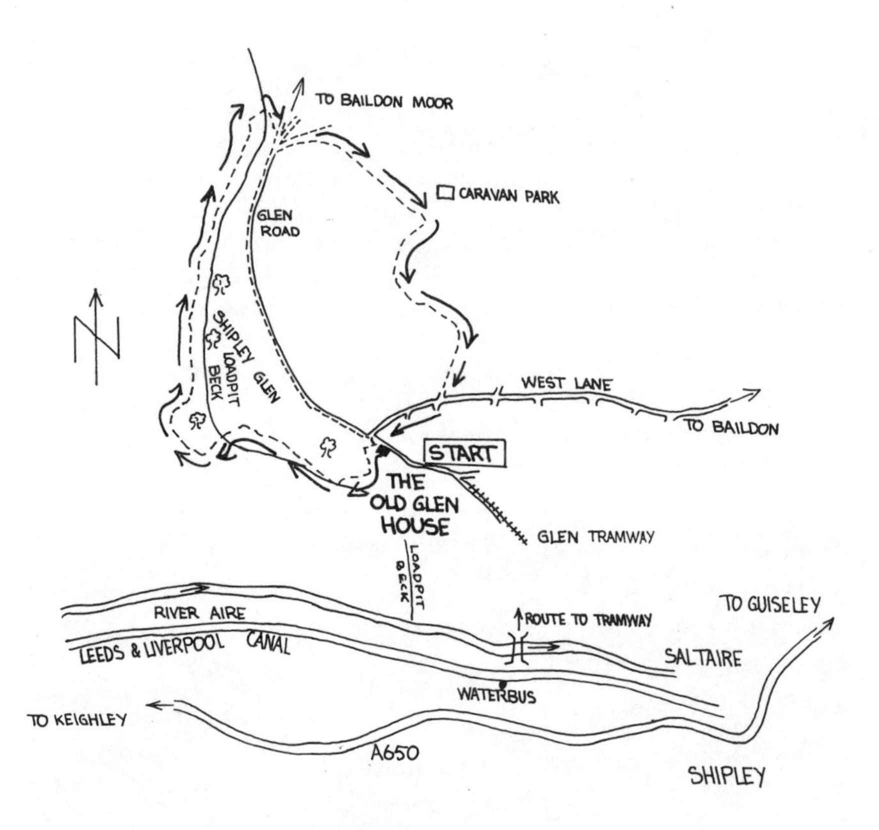

How to get there: The pub is difficult to find. If you approach from Baildon centre, go left at the roundabout along West Lane to the junction with Glen Road and Prod Lane (the pub is just here on the left). Or you can arrive via the Glen Tramway – take the A6038 northbound from Shipley and go first left after crossing the river Aire. Keep left and continue for just under a mile to the large turning circle to the right of the school (adequate parking is available here). The tramway is at the foot of the hill at the edge of the wood. Another option would be to start your journey in Saltaire and travel to the tramway by waterbus, along the canal. (The phone number for the waterbus is 01274 595914).

Parking: There is ample space at the pub.

Length of the walk: 3 miles (4 miles from the start of tramway). OS map: Landranger 104 (inn GR 133388).

The fairy tale qualities of Shipley Glen have bewitched generations of Yorkshire children. They arrive by magic, the cable-operated Glen Tramway giving passengers a delightful introduction to one of the best woodland and moors walks in the county (includes one steep climb).

The tramway runs every day from May to September; at weekends in March, April, October and December; otherwise Sundays only. Telephone: 01274 589010.

The Walk

Leave the pub and go left by the side wall, going left again, following a bridlepath sign between two old gateposts. Proceed along the flagged causeway downhill, swinging right, alongside the wall. Where the path forks, swing right, following the track between two walls through woodland. Swing next left, dropping downhill, and go left between the weir pool and the sluice over a bridge. Veer right, heading up a steep track. Keep going right at the crest by the bungalows and stay on the woodland top path for about ¾ mile. Gradually drop down towards the Loadpit Beck (a feeder of the river Aire used for industrial purposes in times past). Pass the bilberry patch and take the right-hand fork, descending to a bridge over the beck. Go right and swing left between concrete bollards, continuing over open moorland, with a beck to the left, to Glen Road.

Turn right for 100 yards and go left, following the signed 'Crook Farm Caravan Park' access road. There are good views from this vantage point. Just before the park entrance gate, turn right, dropping downhill on a green track and swinging left to an unusual pedestrian gate. Go through, following the arrow markers alongside the bottom perimeter of the caravan park, and go through a gateway (no gate) to a kissing-gate. Go through this, keeping topside of the field, and by the stile in the corner, turn right, following the wall down to a kissing-gate. Go through left, and turn right along the estate road, swinging right and left to West Lane. Turn right to the junction with Prod Lane and go left, back to the pub.

Places of interest nearby
Along Prod Lane are the *Glen Pleasure Grounds* (kiddies' attractions in season). The model village of *Saltaire*, built by the philanthropist Sir Titus Salt across the river, should not be missed.

7 Rawdon
The Princess

Situated on a ridge overlooking the river Aire, busy Rawdon takes its name from a family who settled here after the Norman Conquest. The village was an important hand weaving centre and it has a number of distinguished old buildings, notably Rawdon Hall off Low Green. Its decorative entrance is embellished with carved stone friezes taken from nearby Kirkstall Abbey. Buckstone Rock, situated on the slope near the golf course marks the site of secret convocations during the days of religious persecution. In Cragg Wood is a nursery once famous for the production of orchids.

Having dodged the suitors and the posh frocks, this street corner local is a homely wench. And what a treasure! Buffed up and sparkling, yet unspoilt and unmolested – even the bakelite bell pushes which once summoned the waiters have been preserved – the little princess has a small two-cornered main bar, graced with watercolours, toby jugs and plates, and a delightful snug, hung with evocative Sutcliffe photographs. My kind of girl!

The Princess offers wholesome Yorkshire fare at lunchtime and in the evening. Substantial pies – steak and kidney, corned beef and onion, and meat and potato – are the mainstay of the mid-day menu, backed up with Yorkshire pudding, gammon, and haddock in parsley sauce. The evening choices are extended, dishes including a selection of steaks, lambs' liver and bacon, breast of chicken, pan-fried salmon and several vegetarian alternatives. Children are welcome for meals. Bar-top, there are two hand-pulled real ales – Tetley Bitter and Mild – and Skol, Castlemaine and Carlsberg Export lagers.

The opening times on Monday to Friday are from 12 noon to 3 pm and 5.30 pm to 11 pm, on Saturday from 11 am to 11 pm, and on Sunday from 12 noon to 10.30 pm.

Telephone: 0113 2502495.

How to get there: The inn is beside the A658, Apperley Lane, in Rawdon. Go south from the A658/A65 roundabout (a prestige sports car retailers have their prominent showrooms here).

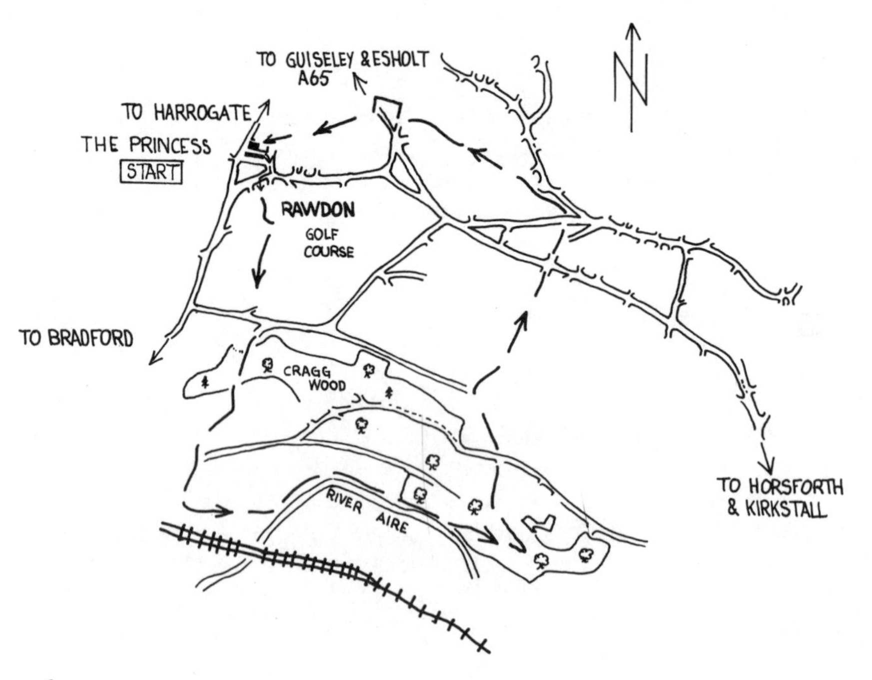

Parking: Parking is restricted to two or three vehicles at the side of the inn, but there is a large car park for customers opposite.

Length of the walk: 4 miles. OS map: Landranger 104 (inn GR 204397).

A fairly hilly walk to the banks of the river Aire. Considering the population of four million people that comes with the Leeds postcode, this superb ramble is astoundingly attractive – and on a bank holiday in the height of summer I saw not a soul! Part of the route follows Victorian trackways, to, in the past, one of Yorkshire's most abused waterways. But the invigorating flashes of kingfishers tell a revival tale.

The Walk

Exiting from the side of the inn, turn left up Back Lombard Street. Swing right and go left on Lombard Street. Turn right on London Lane. Turn right at the main road for 100 yards, down the hill, and go left across the road, following a public footpath sign. Swing left and right and keep going forward, with new housing to the left, to a meadow. Veer left, wallside, for 100 yards and turn 90° right, dropping down alongside the meadow boundary wall.

Keep straight forward along an ancient walled track (so overgrown as to be like a dark tunnel). Cross the access road and swing right, dropping down to the valley bottom. Swing right to the entrance to Acacia Farm and go left along the metalled road, past the cottages to the bend. Veer left, following the public footpath sign (obscured by trees) to the football pitches. Steer left, walking parallel to the railway line, and go through a gap in a wall to the river bank.

Keep on the waterside for about ½ mile, then follow the path as it leaves the river and goes off left through the margins of Cragg Wood. Go through the kissing-gate and arc left by the sewage farm, going left again by the house on a metalled track uphill. At the junction of tracks keep forward, ascending to a footpath marker post. Bear left to the second footpath marker post and go up the steps, then through a gate, aiming left to a stile. Cross and turn right on a path to a road. Cross and mount a stile, going left, following a public footpath sign, left,

Beside the Aire, on the Rawdon walk.

alongside the linear mounds over a field. Cross a metal stile and go right on a tarmac footway, Cliffe Lane, passing the Friends School of 1898 to the right, to the A65.

Cross with care and go straight forward, uphill, along Well Lane to the bend. Keep straight forward again, following the public footpath sign up a flight of steps. Cross a road and pass between the houses, going left up a smaller flight of steps to a road. Turn left on the footway, passing Rawdon Cricket Club, and continue to the premises of Storey Evans Ltd. Turn left, following the public footpath sign. Go through a gap in a wall and keep forward on Peasehill Park. Steering to the right of the triangular parcel of land, keep forward, continuing along the footway, dropping down with the football pitch to the right. Swing left and go down a flight of steps to the A658. Cross and go right for 100 yards, then turn left down a ginnel to the A65.

Turn left and cross the road at the petrol filling station, following a public footpath sign along a track at the side of the park. Swing left to the park entrance and go right on White Lands, then go left for 30 yards on London Lane. Turn right down Princess Street back to the inn.

Places of interest nearby

Just down the road from Rawdon is *Esholt* village, the locale for the TV series 'Emmerdale Farm'. In Rawdon itself is an attraction for dad – a *high performance car showroom* displaying the pride of Porsche and Ferrari. One of the most appealing attractions for the whole family, though, is just down the valley at Kirkstall, with its ruined 12th-century Cistercian Abbey. The former abbey gatehouse is now the *Abbey House Museum* whose centrepiece is a group of rebuilt Victorian streets with shops, cottages and workrooms.

8 Harden
The Malt Shovel

Lovely Harden in its steeply wooded valley was, from the 13th century to the Dissolution, held by the monks of Rievaulx Abbey. In a house still inhabited in Ryecroft hamlet, they brewed beer. They were also active locally in iron smelting. The distinguished Harden Hall built in 1616 as a farmhouse has associations with the Knights of St John. Three small cloth mills were active in the area during the Industrial Revolution. The modern village preserves its 17th-century cottages and, at its crossroads, two fine churches.

As for the inn, this 16th-century gem reeks of times long past. A guardian of the old bridge over Harden Beck, it is a cherished part of local heritage, all mullions and wainscotting, buffed and burnished and dressed with summer flowers. Its fascinating history is chequered, and sometimes dark. Built originally as a farmhouse, the Malt Shovel subsequently saw more colourful employment as a coaching inn, courtroom and prison, and refuge for outlaws. Hanging judges once dispensed justice here, sending the condemned for summary execution on Harden Moor. For some years, one of the bars was used as a cell. The snug preserves a William and Mary fireplace. A third room serves as an attractive and intimate cocktail bar. The patina of old age sits happily alongside modern amenities and a wholesome and traditional home-cooked menu, which includes children's portions. Try the special steak pie, hot roast beef sandwich, giant Yorkshire puddings, or fillet of plaice or haddock. Hand-pulled Tetley bitter is available, together with Castlemaine and Carlsberg Export lagers and draught Guinness. Outside, the inn has an expansive beer garden, delightfully situated overlooking the beck.

The opening times on Monday to Friday are from 12 noon to 3 pm and 5.30 pm to 11 pm. Saturday hours are from 11 am to 11 pm. Sunday opening is from 12 noon to 3 pm and 7.30 pm to 10.30 pm.

Telephone: 01535 272357.

How to get there: This prominent roadside inn is in Harden, south-west of Bingley. Go south from the village on the Wilsden road.

Parking: There is a large car park.

Length of the walk: 2½ miles. OS map: Landranger 104 (inn GR 088378).

Surprising West Yorkshire puts on her most amazing display yet in this torrents and tumbles ramble through unspoilt woodland. Forget the crowds. Let them all converge on Aysgarth while you appreciate Harden's far more spectacular waterfalls in utter peace. A host of wild flowers, dipper and heron hereabouts.

The Walk

Turn right from the inn across the Harden Beck bridge and go left along Goit Stock Lane, following the public footpath sign to 'Goit Stock Wood'. 'Goit' is an old West Riding term for a water channel, usually dug to provide power to a mill. Harden Beck, particularly during the Industrial Revolution, was harnessed for local industry. The evidence is being gradually assimilated into

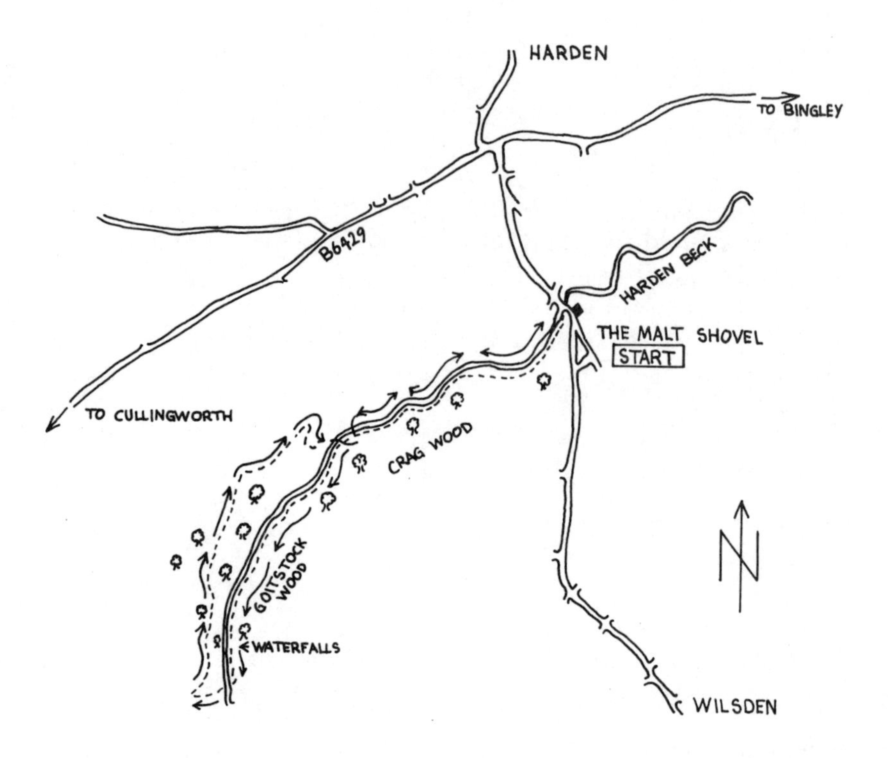

the landscape and only adds to the attractiveness of this exquisite valley. Continue along the lane, keeping straight forward into the Harden Bingley Caravan Park. Go left, following the signpost to 'Waterfalls and Leech Lane'. Continue forward into the woods and gradually drop down towards the waterfall. Continue past the second fall and turn right across the footbridge.

Walk uphill, away from the beck and, when approaching the buildings, look out for yellow and blue arrow-head markers on the right. Follow these, going sharp right through an opening in a wall and swing left by a wall. Cross a stile into a wood, following a yellow arrow marker, and leave the wood through a gap in a wall. Head down the middle of a field, following a line of trees, and cross the Cow House Beck on a footbridge, ascending by a wall. Go through a gap by a gate, following a yellow arrow-head marker, swinging right and dropping down

A waterfall in Goitstock wood.

towards the caravan site. Walk under power lines, continuing through a gap by a gate and, after 30 yards, swing sharp right on a track downhill into the site. Swing left by the conifer hedge and go left for 20 yards, then right, following the public footpath sign. Go left over the beck on the footbridge and then left again, retracing the outward route back to the inn.

Places of interest nearby

North of Harden is the *St Ives Country Estate*, incorporating wooded grounds (outstanding rhododendrons), play areas, a nature trail and fishing ponds.

9 Aberford
The Swan Hotel

Coaches and six once thundered into the courtyard of the old Swan, a commodious and welcoming hostelry which has lost none of its character and bustle despite being deserted by the re-routed Great North Road. The village of Aberford with its splendid almshouses, church, ancient bridge over the Cock Beck (children's play area close by) and pine furniture showrooms has a wealth of local attractions for all ages. And, the six-bedroomed hotel claims to offer the longest and most varied menu in the country, the list extending to over 500 dishes!

Furnished with an eclectic assembly of taxidermal specimens, old bottles, pictures, prints and rustic paraphernalia, the three interconnecting bars and the upstairs Cygnet restaurant serve a globe-trotting cuisine, ranging from steak and kidney pie to Peking aromatic duck. Do the United Nations dining chambers have more choice . . . Hungarian salmon, Mexican chilli prawns, Singapore seafood curry, Indonesian mixed platter, Bengali kebabs, American widgeon aromatic, New Zealand rib eye steak, Portuguese chicken piri piri, moussaka Greek-style and veal escalope Italiano? A self-service carvery operates from Monday to Saturday and children and vegetarians have their own menus. As for drinks, Tetley Bitter is available on handpump, alongside guests such as Castle Eden and Flowers IPA. There is a wide range of lagers, ciders and wines. Popular barbecues and children's activities are organised in the attractive garden during the summer months.

An old post horse sign at the Swan Hotel.

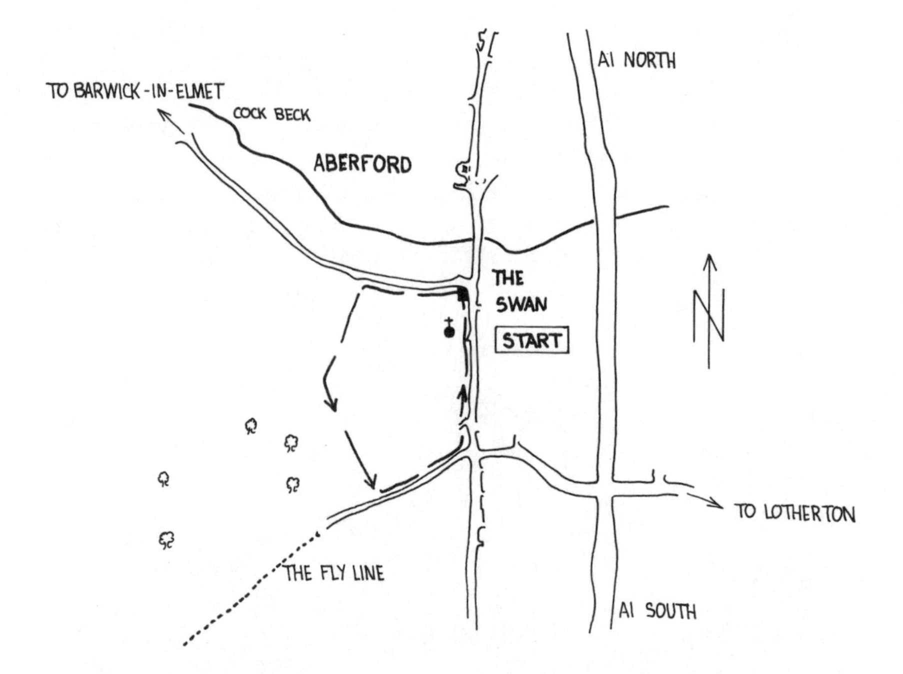

Food is available whenever the bar is open – Monday to Saturday from 11 am to 3 pm and 6 pm to 11 pm, and Sunday from 12 noon to 3 pm and 7 pm to 10.30 pm.

Telephone: 0113 2813205.

How to get there: The hotel is on the old Great North Road at the junction with Barwick Road in Aberford, east of Leeds. It is easily reached from the A1.

Parking: There is a large courtyard – under the supervision of an attendant at busy times.

Length of the walk: 2 miles. OS map: Landranger 105 (inn GR 434373).

An easy stroll through historic parkland developed by the dynastic Gascoigne family, returning along the sylvan course of an abandoned mineral railway – the 'Fly Line'. A succession of architectural gems and oddities, fragments of industrial archaeology and specimen trees and wild flowers pack this walk with interest.

The Walk

Exit from the side entrance and turn right through the courtyard. Swing right and continue to Barwick Road. Turn left for about 100 yards and opposite the estate house [notice the symbolic luce's (pike's) head above the doorway, part of the Gascoigne coat of arms – see the full armorial splendour in the stained glass windows in nearby Barwick church] turn left along Parlington Drive.

Continue along the estate road towards the triumphal arch in the distance. This was erected by the Gascoignes in 1783 to commemorate 'Liberty in N. America triumphant'. About 250 yards before the arch, turn left, following a yellow arrow marker on a post, and continue along a fenceline, downhill over open pasture.

Ascend to a stile and cross onto the route of the old 'Fly Line'. This private branch of the Leeds-Selby line was opened in 1835 to haul coal from the Gascoigne mines in Garforth to Aberford for onward transportation north along the A1. At this point it is well worth detouring right for ½ mile or so along the track to view the Dark Arch, built to screen the now demolished Parlington Hall from the view of coal carts. This is not strictly a tunnel. The trains went round it!

To continue the walk, turn left, go through a gate and drop down to the road. (The exquisite, Gothic inspired Gascoigne almshouses are 250 yards to the right.) Turn left along the village street, passing St Ricarius's church, back to the hotel.

Places of interest nearby

Across the Cock Beck is another fascinating old inn – the *Arabian Horse* – the only such named establishment in the land. Also worthy of a visit, best seen west of the village, is *Becca Banks*, three Iron Age entrenchments interspersed by ditches. A must for children is the excellent *Lotherton Hall Bird Garden* (free entry). Turn right from the hotel and go left under the A1 for about a mile.

10 Whitkirk, Leeds
The Brown Cow

With its 15th-century church and cluster of 18th-century cottages, Whitkirk, on the eastern outskirts of Leeds, is an attraction in its own right. The real crowd puller in the area, however, is nearby Temple Newsam Park, the destination of this walk.

A big and spacious roadhouse conversion, the Brown Cow occupies a prominent site on the main road, opposite St Mary's. Decorated in country manor style – a successful blend of stained glass, rustic bygones, prints and mock bookcases – the inn has two comfortable linear bars and an upstairs restaurant part of which is reserved for non-smokers. Facilities include a stair lift for disabled customers and a fenced off beer garden/children's play area. Served under Tetley's corporate 'Porterhouse Restaurant' banner, the extensive menu offers value-for-money, three-course specials, with main courses including fillet of cod, Cajun chicken, steaks and harvest vegetable and cheese crumble. There are also 'country classics', such as beef and Tetley bake and Lincolnshire duck with orange sauce, and a good range of vegetarian alternatives. The Sunday lunches are very popular. Children have a separate menu. In addition to draught Tetley Bitter, Mild and Imperial, the inn serves guest beers, Carlsberg and Castlemaine lagers and draught Guinness.

The opening times on Monday to Saturday are from 11.30 am to 11 pm. Sunday hours are from 12 noon to 3 pm and 7 pm to 10.30 pm.

Telephone: 0113 2646112.

How to get there: The inn is on Selby Road, the A63, 3 miles from Leeds.

Parking: Ample facilities are available at the inn.

Length of the walk: 2½ miles. OS map: Landranger 104 (inn GR 364336).

A captivating ramble – through a churchyard, along a path to a secret garden, over 900 acres of heroic landscape to one of the finest mansions in the North of England, and back, over greensward to the inn.

Owned and managed by Leeds City Council, Temple Newsam estate comprises a magnificent Carolean house (entry fee), a working farm and rural bygones attraction for children (free entry) and extensive formal gardens and lawns. For details of opening times, telephone: 0113 2647321.

The Walk

Leaving the front entrance of the inn, cross the road and go through the lychgate of the parish church, continuing left through the churchyard. There are a number of inscribed tombstones in the grounds, and an interior monument commemorates the famous lighthouse builder John Smeaton.

Continue straight ahead along the footway of Colton Road for 250 yards, going left, crossing the road and passing between the concrete bollards. Keep going along the footpath for 150 yards and turn right by the third lamp standard, through a gap in a hedge, to find a footpath. Walk on, keeping left along the edge of the trees and veer left into the wood, keeping streamside. Continue on an ash track, go through a kissing-gate and,

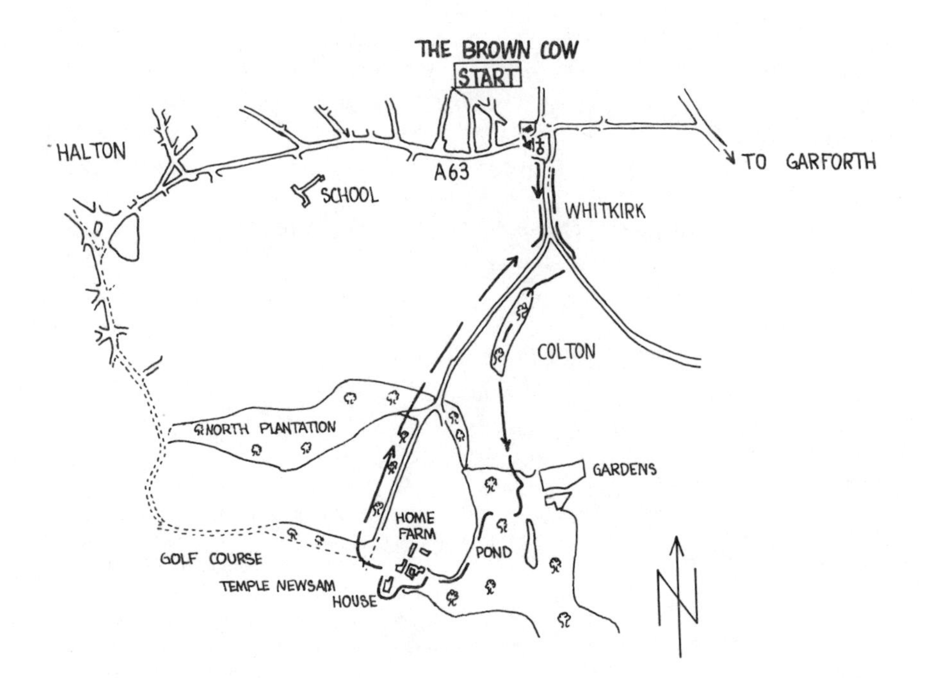

keeping straight forward, follow the sign to 'Temple Newsam'.

At the end of the shaled track, enter the estate grounds and turn left on a tarmac footpath, swinging right, uphill to the Rose Garden. This prize-winning area shows the art of the cottage garden at its best; but see also the tropical displays in the greenhouse – a wonderful retreat from the cold in the winter months.

Turn right through the ornamental gates (notice the Knights Templar motif) and drop down, going left along the side of the ornamental lake to the trip-trap bridge (according to my children, the home – underneath – of an ugly troll!). Turn right across the wooden bridge and swing left along the footpath alongside the rhododendrons.

Swing right uphill towards the house and Home Farm. This former estate farm exhibits a wide range of animals – some rare breeds – and has extensive farm implements and machinery exhibits.

Continue uphill to the house and notice the old laundry to the

An unusual gravestone in St Mary's churchyard, Whitkirk.

right (free entry). Make a circuit of the house, turning left and right and right again. The 1788 balustrade inscription along the gutter line reads: 'ALL GLORY AND PRAISE BE GIVEN TO GOD THE FATHER THE SON AND HOLY GHOST ON HIGH PEACE ON EARTH GOOD WILL TOWARDS MEN HONOUR AND TRUE ALLEGIANCE TO OUR GRACIOUS KING LOVING AFFECTION AMONGST HIS SUBJECTS HEALTH AND PLENTY BE WITHIN THIS HOUSE'. Temple Newsam has a wealth of architectural and historical interest and contains one of the finest publicly owned collections of English decorative art outside London.

Keep going straight forward, veering left to walk through the third avenue of trees. At the end of the avenue, cross the car park and continue forward between the brick pillars, onto the playing fields. Head for the church, going to the right of the Whitkirk Wanderers football pitch, and walk on towards the white bungalows. Rejoin Colton Road and turn left, back to the inn.

11 Oxenhope
The Dog and Gun

Sharing the heights with lapwings and distant windmills, this stone-built, flagged-roof redoubt stands at a lonely junction overlooking Oxenhope. In a remote Y-shaped valley only 9 miles from Bradford, Oxenhope is an invigorating village surrounded by heathered hills and moorlands. In the 19th century the local economy was based on worsted production at 20 local mills. The rugged character of the village is preserved in over 70 listed buildings.

A former yeoman's cottage preserving ancient windows and an indoor well, which is now exposed and imaginatively floodlit, the Dog and Gun has one long bar and two small side rooms for more formal dining. An open fire adds to the snugness on winter days. Relax and enjoy the view, choosing from a surprising menu which mixes old favourites like steak and kidney pie and grilled plaice with more unusual dishes such as a warm salad of black pudding, mushrooms and bacon and coq au vin. Children have separate choices. Timothy Taylo

Arriving at Oxenhope station. (Courtesy of Roy Hartley)

championship-winning beers – hand-pulled Golden Best, Landlord and Best Bitter – take pride of place on the bar. Ayingerbrau lager and Murphy's stout are also on offer. It gets a little draughty at these altitudes but a small outside seating area is provided for customers who want to drink in the view.

The opening hours on Monday to Saturday are from 11.30 am to 3 pm and 5.30 pm to 11 pm. Sunday opening is from 12 noon to 3 pm and 7 pm to 11 pm.

Telephone: 01535 643159.

How to get there: The pub is south-east of Oxenhope village, midway between Oxenhope and Denholme, and at the junction of the B6141 with Trough Lane.

Parking: There is parking opposite the pub, with nearby overspill facilities.

Length of the walk: 2¼ miles. OS map: Landranger 104 (inn GR 048343).

A moorland flirtation. Fresh air by the lungful (an obvious place for windmills!) along centuries-old trackways, parts of which are now incorporated into the Brontë Way.

The Walk

Take the quiet Sawood Lane immediately opposite the pub, walking uphill. Swing left and right, passing Cobling Farm, and veer right to a gate. Go through and keep going ahead, following the signpost 'Brontë Way – Oxenhope 1½ miles' for a short distance on a metalled road. Merge with a track at the entrance to Thornton Moor Reservoir and go through a gate, following a blue arrow marker. Continue to a three-directional signpost and turn right, following the sign 'Brontë Way'.

Drop downhill left and swing right, following the well-distributed arrow markers, towards Leeming Reservoir. Cross the ladder stile over the conduit and continue the descent to a bridge in the bottom. Turn sharp right through the metal gate and, keeping to the right of the hillock, swing left on the broad, green track adjacent to the reservoir. Go right through a wicket gate and continue between the cottages to the road.

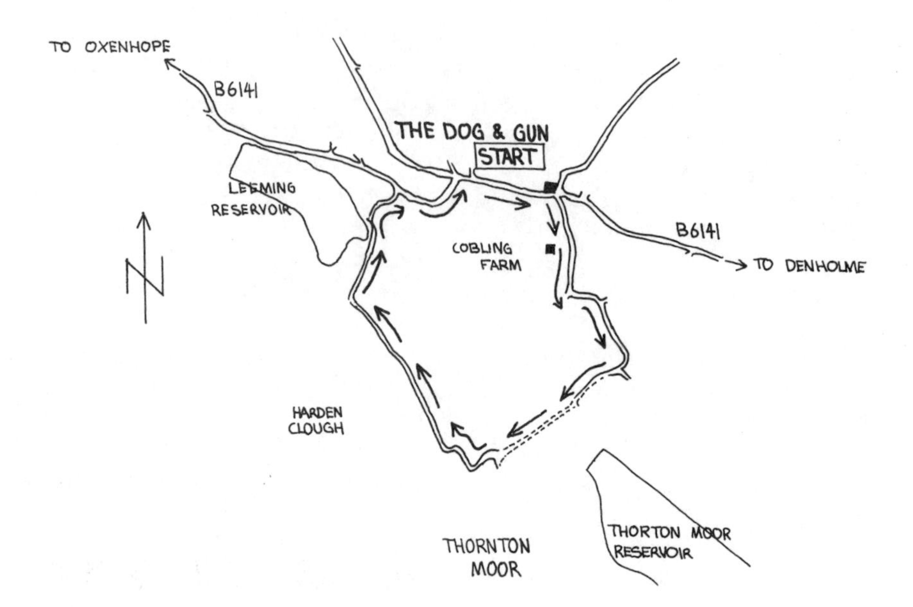

Turn right (this is a quiet road but there are no footways, so caution!) uphill, back to the inn.

Places of interest nearby

The main attraction in Oxenhope is the *Keighley and Worth Valley Railway* – Britain's last remaining complete branch line – operating steam trains every weekend throughout the year and daily in summer. The railway which was made famous as the locational setting for the film *The Railway Children* was originally built in 1867. Following closure in 1961, it was bought from British Railways and re-opened as a private venture in 1968. The romance of the Brontës is just a station away at *Haworth*. Also in Oxenhope are trackside picnic and viewing areas and a museum.

12 Colden
The New Delight Inn

The clatter of the cloggy processions to the mills has long since faded on the wind, once-industrialised Colden regressing into pastoral solitude. Only its remodelled 1790s alehouse and a hamlet of cottage conversions remain to enjoy the fresh moorland airs and the long distance views.

Hard by Jack Bridge, the New Delight Inn is aptly named, having undergone a sensitive refurbishment, providing a rare combination of modern facilities and a traditional interior and atmosphere. Freed from accumulations of paint and plaster – the hacking revealed two secret rooms – the bare inn walls have been matched in the public bar with flagstones, an open fire and a log-burning stove, a suspended collection of Tilley lamps adding to the cosiness. The carpeted lounge bar equally invites dalliance, the sleepy tick of a wall clock, the soft furnishings, the excellent ale and food and panoramic views of advancing rain clouds conspiring to induce a strange lethargy . . .

The inn menu will particularly appeal to walkers and campers, consisting of wholesome Yorkshire fare such as steak and kidney pie. Children are welcome for meals. Owned by real ale enthusiasts, the New Delight serves a wide range of handpulled beers, including Mansfield Riding and Old Baily, Adnams Broadside, Old Speckled Hen, Bombardier and Old Fart. Carlsberg and Stella Artois lagers are also available. The inn has four letting bedrooms and an adjacent camping field (tents only) with a shower block.

The opening times on Monday to Saturday are from 11 am to 11 pm. Sunday hours are from 12 noon to 10.30 pm.

Telephone: 01422 842795.

How to get there: Not a straight forward proposition. The most direct access from Hebden Bridge (by the church and through Mytholm and on to Blackshaw Head) is, in the first ½ mile, narrow and precipitous – even for 4-wheel-drive vehicles! A better route is via the Heptonstall road but even this has a complication for motorists approaching from the east on the A646. Such is the impossibly tight turning circle at the junction of the A646 and the Heptonstall road that right turns are prohibited, cars being signed 300 yards onwards to a purpose-built turning area. Return along the A646 and go left up the hill. Ignore the next left turn into Heptonstall, continuing up the hill. Swing left and go right into Slack, forking left, downhill, into Colden.

Parking: Space is available outside the inn and adjacent to the nearby camping area.

Length of the walk: 4½ miles. OS map: Landranger 103 (inn GR 963283).

The Colden Clough clothing industry may have disappeared, but not so its legacy, the web of packhorse routes and flagged causeways accessing a well-timbered valley almost gorge-like in its acclivity. This splendid wuthering heights walk follows ancient trails, passing an eerie smokeless chimney and the remnants of the old mill on the way to the citadel village of Heptonstall, cobbled and still remarkably preserved and unspoilt. The paths on this route are very steep in places and the walk is not recommended for youngsters under 10 years old.

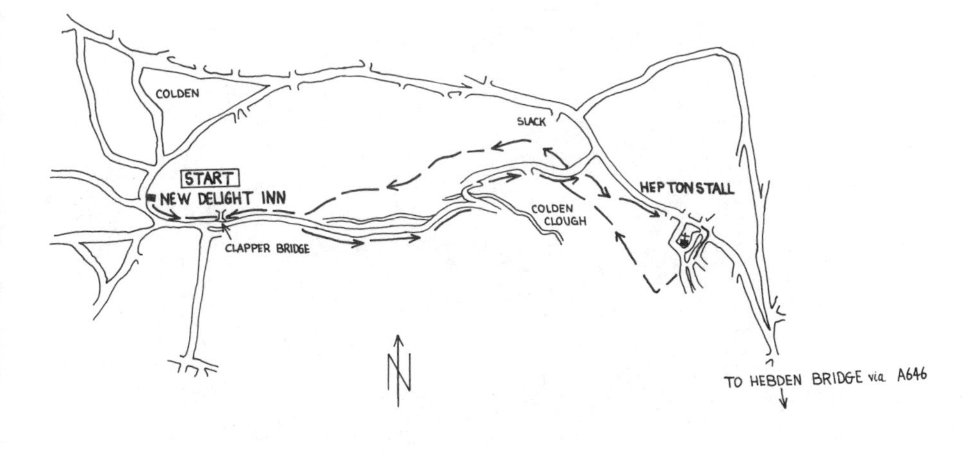

The Walk
Turn right from the inn for 50 yards and go left, following a bridleway sign, on a rough track known as Hudson Mill Road. Gradually drop down towards the stream in Colden Clough. After about 1 mile, at the junction of trackways, go sharp left, almost heading back towards Colden for 150 yards on a track and swing right over the stream on a bridge. Keep left along the cobbled way, climbing up and swinging left after 50 yards.

Swing right, continuing uphill along the metalled Lumb Road. Swing left on Green Lane, passing Windy Harbour Farm and immediately go right at the side of the building (route not marked), going left through a small gate into a meadow. Turn immediately right, following the wall to the corner, and go through the gap, steering diagonally left along the causeway to a gap in a wall. Go through and turn right into Heptonstall, a village that once hummed to the sound of hand-looms. The last weaver here died in 1902, having earned a weekly wage of 6s 6d.

Proceed along Towngate and pass the old pump and the Cloth Hall of 1545, swinging right just after Northgate.

To the right, in the centre of the village, are twin churches, one ruined and dating from the 13th century. The new church, which was completed in 1854, incorporates relics from its predecessor and houses a fine Italian painting of the Last Supper. The adjacent churchyard with its serried rows of

The old clapper bridge at Colden Clough.

tombstones is said to contain 100,000 bodies. The grave of the notorious coiner David Hartley, who was hanged in 1770 for counterfeiting, lies near the porch. Nearby is the 17th-century former grammar school, now converted to a museum.

Proceed along Hepton Drive and go left along the track, swinging right between the dry-stone walls bisecting the new development. At the end of the path, turn right, keeping to the winding ridge's top track for about ½ mile to rejoin Green Lane.

Go left, downhill, for 100 yards and veer slightly right, following the yellow arrow marker, keeping forward to the summit. At the telegraph pole, continue going forward, following the yellow arrow marker through a gap in a dry-stone wall, continuing on a causeway. Go through a second gap in a dry-stone wall and walk on to the right of a farmhouse. Some 50 yards after this building, veer left towards Colden Clough and swing right, following the yellow arrow marker. Go through a gate and continue wallside to a second gate. Go through this and proceed on a causeway for 100 yards, looking out on the left for a pole in a gap between a wall. Go left through the gap, swinging diagonally left downhill towards the trees on a causeway. Cross a wall and keep forward, dropping down through bracken, towards the stream. Turn right along the streamside for 35 yards and go left over the clapper bridge.

This beautifully simple bridge is constructed from four monumental slabs of stone. Part of the parapet is inscribed. Is the date 1830?

Swing right, climbing up to Hudson Mill Road, then turn right and go right again, back to the inn.

Places of interest nearby

A visit to the New Delight combined with a walk to nearby Heptonstall can easily consume a half day but leave time to enjoy the attractions of *Hebden Bridge*. With Calder Valley Cruising you can take a horse-drawn boat to a number of local destinations – *World of the Honey Bee* exhibition, *Walkley's Clog Mill* and *Todmorden Market* (motor boat only). In addition to a number of specialist shops, Hebden Bridge can also offer a chamber of horrors, *Hebden Crypt*.

13 Shibden
The Shibden Mill Inn

For 800 years, the Shibden Brook earned its corn in a tranquil dell north of Halifax. Today the flow tinkles on, freed from the constriction of goits and spillways, and although the mighty water wheel has gone, the miller's tale lives on in a remarkable building.

With architectural features dating from the 17th century, the picturesque Shibden Mill Inn incorporates the old miller's house. It has an attractive public bar and an adjoining restaurant with exposed timbers and a feature Jacobean fireplace. Quality, big portioned bar meals are available every lunchtime and evening. Standard dishes such as Yorkshire puddings, bacon and cheese baguettes, sirloin and gammon steaks and scampi are complemented by daily blackboard specials – typically, oaty trout fillets, deep fried Brie and cranberry sauce, Devonshire duck and peaches, chicken and ham mille-feuille, pork and filo pastry parcels and kidneys turbigo. The restaurant fare features julienne of fillet beef, salmon finished with a net of puff pastry, chicken St Frances (filled with ham and garlic cheese), orange and almond stuffed lamb and marinated pork and pineapple skewer. Children have a special menu. The inn serves a selection of hand-pulled real ales – Old Mill, Timothy Taylor Landlord, Nelly Dean and Black Sheep. The lager alternatives are McEwan's and Carlsberg Export. Six en-suite letting bedrooms are available, together with a banqueting suite for functions. The inn has a pleasant patio area.

The opening times on Monday to Friday are from 11.30 am to 3.30 pm and 5.30 pm to 11 pm. Saturday and Sunday hours are 11 am to 11 pm.

Telephone: 01422 365840.

How to get there: The inn is in Shibden, 3 miles north-east of Halifax. The best access is along Kell Lane, going north from the A58 Godley Lane/Leeds Road junction (at the Stump Cross public house). Turn next left along Blake Hill.

Parking: A large car park is available, and there is additional parking 20 yards along the adjacent lane.

Halifax Piece Hall. (Courtesy of Calderdale Leisure Services Department)

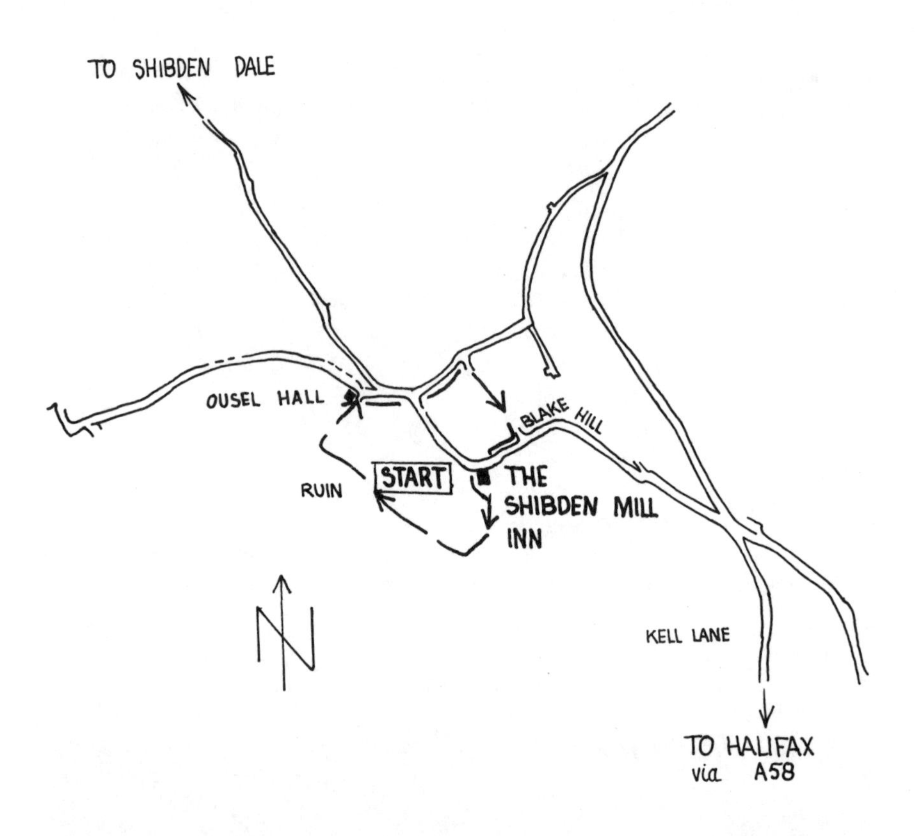

Length of the walk: Just 1 mile (further, more extended, walks can be enjoyed close by in Shibden Dale). OS map: Landranger 104 (inn GR 102273).

A short, circular appreciation of a fine watering hole (the inn is hardly ever out of sight!), across a hillside and returning along an old packhorse trail. A good spot for blackberrying at the end of the summer.

The Walk

Turn left from the inn along Horley Green Lane, going over the brook and swinging right. Bear left past the farmhouse for 50 yards and turn right over a stile, climbing up, with a wall to the left, to the field corner. Cross a stile and climb up onto an embankment, then swing right over hummocky ground. Follow the lower contours of the hillside at first (it doesn't matter exactly where), generally arcing left and gradually ascending. Pass a ruin to the left and head for a stile ahead. Cross the stile into a coppice and swing left. Turn sharp right over the next stile and continue on a path, dropping down, wallside, to a stile near Ousel Hall. Cross the stile and turn right, downhill, along the cobbled lane. Cross the bridge over the brook, swing right and go left along the signposted Dam Head and then go right along the signposted Dicken – an old packhorse causeway. Turn next right along the lane, back to the inn.

Places of interest nearby

Shibden Hall is an obvious destination for visitors to the area. Part of the period mansion dates from 1420. It contains a fascinating collection of 17th and 18th-century furniture and household objects. Adults should not fail to explore Halifax's *Piece Hall*, one of Europe's most outstanding 18th-century buildings. Its carefully restored arcades, galleries and courtyard were originally built for purveying 'pieces' of cloth, a trade carried on by 315 merchants. The building now houses speciality shops and three weekly markets. For children, Britain's first hands-on museum is a must. *Eureka!* in Halifax has received many major awards and is in every way a winner.

14 Pontefract
The Counting House

Shakespeare refers to this ancient citadel town as 'Bloody Pomfret', the sanguine epithet deriving from the mysterious death in 1400 of King Richard II in Pontefract Castle – the destination for this walk. The town has a fascinating hub of medieval streets and some fine buildings, notably St Giles' church, the Butter Cross, the Town Hall and the Market Hall.

Built when Shakespeare was just a lad, the splendid half-timbered Counting House is one of the oldest surviving vernacular buildings in Pontefract. Dating from the 16th century and monumentally ribbed with oak beams, scarf-jointed and fixed with dowel pegging, it had seen prior use as a warehouse, a malting house and twin cottages before being imaginatively converted into a pub in 1994. Both linear ground and first floor bars ooze atmosphere, the reverential treatment of ancient timbers, old fireplaces, stone flagging and dusky nooks and corners preserving a soul that comes complete with a trio of resident ghosts. Who needs a Globe Theatre? Henry V could have no more genuine setting than this – but come quick before some Yank ships it lock, stock and barrels to the States!

The pub offers a standard bar menu, which includes minted lamb chops, fried cod, beef and mushroom pie, chilli con carne, hot roast beef sandwiches and giant Yorkshire puddings. Children have their own choices. Three hand-pulled ales – Tetley, Theakston and Flowers – plus a guest are available, alongside Stella and Carlsberg lagers and draught Guinness. The Counting House has an outdoor seating area, to the side.

The opening hours on Monday to Saturday are from 11 am to 3 pm and 5.30 pm to 11 pm. Sunday hours are from 12 noon to 3 pm and 7 pm to 10.30 pm.

Telephone: 01977 600388.

How to get there: Pontefract is immediately south of the M62 motorway and is easily accessible from junction 32, along the A639. The pub is conveniently located off Corn Market.

Parking: Leave your car in one of the central 'pay and display' car parks.

Length of the walk: 1½ miles. OS map: Landranger 105 (inn GR 455220).

Pontefract castle.

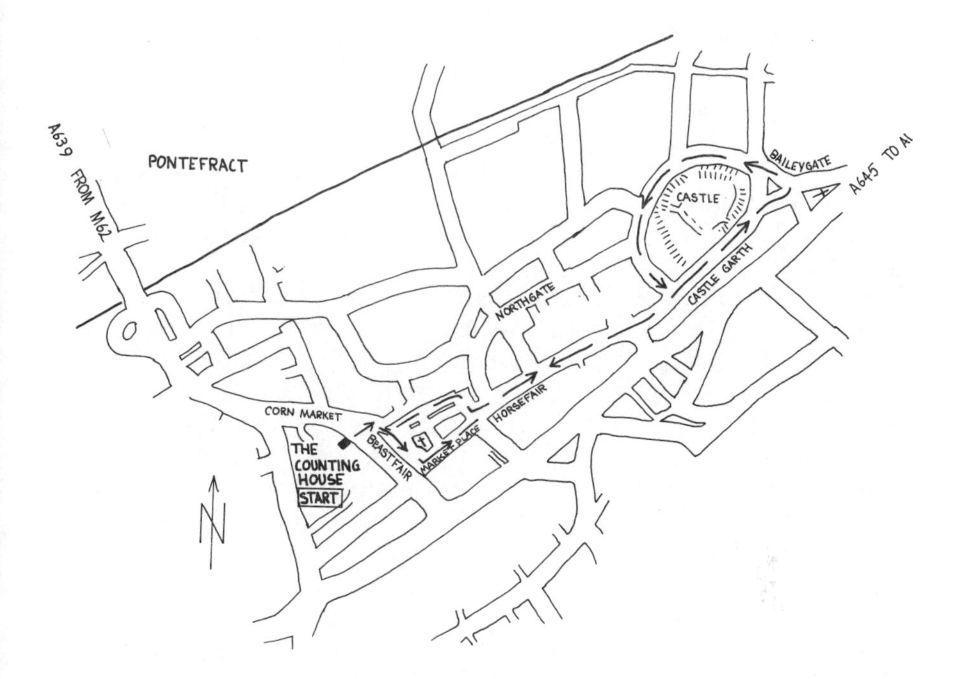

A historical town centre walk through pedestrian precincts and along pavements to the remains of Pontefract castle, once the mightiest fortress in all Europe. The castle was largely demolished after the Civil War but beguiling fragments remain.

There is free admission to the grounds, which are open from 8.30 am to 7 pm (or dusk) on Monday to Friday, and 10.30 am to 4.30 pm on Saturday and Sunday. The visitor centre is open from 10.30 am to 12.30 pm and 1.30 pm to 4.30 pm between April and October, and from 2 pm to 4 pm between November and March.

The Walk

Turn left from the pub down Swales Yard into Corn Market. Keep straight forward across the road and turn right down Shoe Market, keeping to the right of St Giles' church and the Butter Cross. Go left along the pedestrianised Market Place, noticing the magnificent bull head carvings on the Market Hall. Pass the Liquorice Bush pub (the unique local brew, Three Sieges strong stout, which is flavoured with liquorice, may be sampled here) and go to the left of the Town Hall down Bridge Street. Continue along Horsefair for about 300 yards and, at the bend, keep going forward, following the signposted route to the castle, on Micklegate. Proceed along Castle Garth to the castle.

Inside the grounds, see the Keep, the Swillington Tower and the underground Magazine, where prisoners carved their names into the cell walls, and follow the castle's tempestuous history in the visitor centre.

After examining the site take a circuit of the perimeter, going left from the entrance on Castle Garth, dropping down and forking right on Booths. On the left are the exposed remains of an Anglo Saxon church. Cross the road ahead (Tanners Row) and visit All Saints' church. Ruined during the Civil War, it was partially restored in 1838. Returning, go right on North Baileygate, passing the massive foundations of the Swillington Tower, and arc left, going left on Spink Lane, to get back to the castle entrance.

Turn right, returning along Micklegate and Horsefair and, opposite the Town Hall, swing right on Salter Row. Turn left opposite the museum and go through the alley between the Cartners Arms and the Beastfair Vaults, turning right and left back to the pub.

Places of interest nearby

Pontefract Museum (free admission) in Salter Row is housed in a 1900s building decorated in Art Nouveau style. Exhibits chart the history of the local liquorice industry and there is a fine collection of siege coins minted to pay the troops during the three Civil War sieges of the castle. A 17th-century painting shows the castle unmolested.

Norland
The Hobbit

A scattering of solidly-built, old stone houses with spectacular views make up the hamlet of Norland. Most have been lovingly converted, their characteristically long windows were originally designed to allow the maximum penetration of light for weaving. On Norland Moor is the infamous Gallows Pole Hill where dozens of convicted criminals were executed.

Gazing out at half the Pennines, the century-old Hobbit hugs the contours like a petrified cat. Converted from three delvers' cottages into an alehouse and in recent years to a popular hotel, it offers up-to-the-minute attractions, with 22 en-suite bedrooms and an 80 cover restaurant, as well as conference and function facilities. It also has a bar/bistro, Bilbo's – L-shaped, with panoramic views – which is very popular with walkers. Its extensive and wide-ranging international menu includes New Zealand mussels, Chinese hors d'oeuvre, tandoori chicken, pork italienne and a range of pizzas with a Hobbit connection ('Gandalf the Wizard' for example, uses mozzarella, tomato, peppers, mushrooms, onion and olives). Prominent amongst the list of traditional meals are home-made pies, steaks, giant Yorkshire puddings and haddock. The main dish of the day will be something like pan-fried kidneys or broccoli and blue cheese pie. Children have their own menu. Good value specials (for two persons) are served on Monday to Thursday evenings. Friday and Saturday nights are lively, offering music and dancing, with a late licence until 2 am. Murder and Mystery evenings and other themed events are a regular feature. Matching the interesting menu is a medley of liquid refreshments – hand-pulled bitters from Courage, Ruddles and John Smith's, Chestnut mild, Foster's, Carlsberg and Budweiser lagers and draught Guinness.

The bar is open on Monday to Saturday from 12 noon to 11 pm (later for food). Sunday hours are from 12 noon to 10.30 pm.

Telephone: 01422 832202.

How to get there: The hotel is on Hob Lane at Norland, south of Sowerby Bridge. It can be reached from the A6026 or the B6113, turning off the moorland road, downhill, near the golf course.

Parking: The hotel has extensive car parking facilities on three sides.

Length of the walk: 3½ miles. OS map: Landranger 104 (inn GR 058226).

From the Ryburn valley bottom to the heights of Norland Moor with hardly a level yard. Not for the short of puff! This fascinating route takes in old lanes, a disused railway line, cobbled causeways and a heathery trod with fine views of Sowerby Bridge and the Wainhouse Tower.

The Walk

Turn right from the Hobbit and go left, following the public footpath sign, swinging right downhill and going left and left again. Turn right along Goose Nest Lane and drop down to the fork, going left for 200 yards. Turn right, following the signposted permissive bridleway to Stansfield Mill, downhill. At

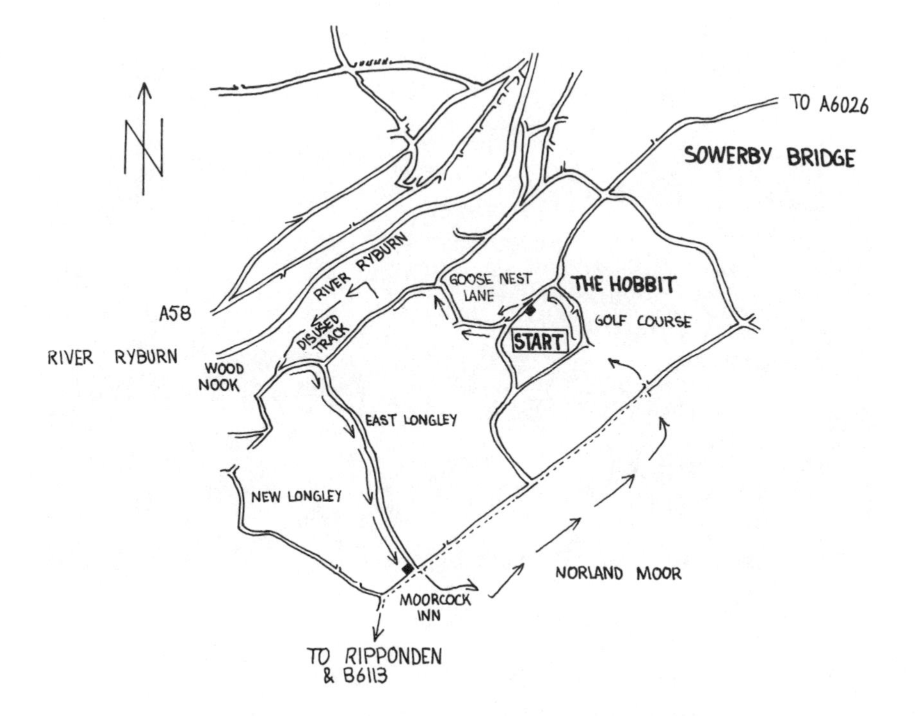

the old railway bridge, swing to the right and go sharp left under the span, along the line of the disused track. Walk on to the next overbridge and go under, turning immediately right and scrambling up the bank. Complete a U-turn and cross the bridge, walking uphill to Wood Nook.

Turn left and go next right, ascending on a cobbled lane, keeping forward on the metalled road to the Moorcock Inn. Cross the road and walk onto the moor on the distinctive path, taking the left-hand fork on the summit edge, through the heather. Continue past the metalled fencing for about ¼ mile and go under pylon wires before turning left to the road. Cross and turn right for 10 yards, then go left, following a public footpath signposted to Sowerby Bridge, across the golf course. Weave to the left by the clubhouse and proceed on the access to the road. Turn right and turn left, back to the inn.

Norland Moor. (Courtesy of Calderdale Leisure Services Department)

Places of interest nearby

Nearby *Sowerby Bridge* has a number of interesting attractions centred around the Calder and the marina. A slalom course on the river has been set out for canoeists. Several historic warehouses on the waterfront have been restored and converted – they still retain their unusual 'shipping holes', which allowed barges access to the inside of the buildings. Stows of Sowerby, a mill shop operating two of the last remaining power shuttle looms in Calderdale (located at Lower Snape Farm, west of Sowerby Bridge centre – from Town Gate go along Higham and Dob Lane towards Steep Lane), sells traditionally woven rugs, shawls, hand-weaving yarns and wools. To the north-east of Sowerby is the prominent *Wainhouse Tower*, one of the north's most striking architectural follies. Built in 1875 to a height of 253 ft, it served as a dyeworks chimney. It has a central staircase of 403 steps and elaborate viewing balconies, and is open for public ascents on holiday weekends.

16 Rishworth
The Royal Hotel

Sandwiched between brooding moors in the valley of the river Ryburn, Rishworth is best known for its independent public school, a grand complex of mainly Georgian buildings. The village grew up around its great corn mill which was adapted for cotton manufacture in 1836. Rishworth is close to the M62 but it suffers little from traffic intrusion and there are many pleasant walks in the area particularly near the Ryburn, Baitings and Ringstone Edge reservoirs.

The imposing three-storied Royal shares its roadside frontage with the famous Rishworth School. Both buildings date from the 18th century, the ivy clad inn once serving as a posting and meeting house. The comfortable and unusual Royal has three distinctive bars, each crammed with bygones and curios – naval paintings, ships' models, swords, Victorian prints, corner cupboards, statues, vases and shells.

The eclectic theme extends to the extensive home-made menu. Standard dishes such as steak and kidney pie, steak and mushroom pie, grilled gammon and lamb cutlets are supplemented by blackboard specials – typically, chicken breast stuffed with cheese and bacon in a Provençale sauce and chicken and ham tagliatelle. The choice of sweets is equally varied, ranging from mille-feuille to sticky toffee pudding. Children are welcome for meals. Beer drinkers can select from six hand-pulled bitters, John Smith's, Ruddles, Ruddles County, Webster's and Green Label and Courage Directors. Foster's, Holsten and Carlsberg lagers and Guinness are also on tap. Accommodation is available in six rooms and the hotel has a large function room, a terrace and a beer garden.

The opening times are from 11 am to 11 pm on Monday to Saturday. Sunday hours are from 12 noon to 3 pm and 6.30 pm to 10.30 pm.

Telephone: 01422 822382.

How to get there: The inn is on the A672. Leave the M62 at junction 22 and go north-east to Rishworth.

Parking: Adequate parking is available at the inn, or on the road.

Length of the walk: 2½ miles. OS map: Landranger 110 (inn GR 035185).

Every step is packed with interest on this easy amble – old schools, water meadows beside Yorkshire's least known river, mills, goits and a palace!

The Walk

Turn right from the inn on the footway alongside the A672 and pass the war memorial. Turn next right on Rishworth New Road. Walk uphill for 200 yards and go left just before the 'Hill Croft' sign, up a flight of steps (no footpath sign), passing an old churchyard. Turn right on Godly Lane and at the junction turn right for 10 yards and go left along the footpath known as Shaw Lane. To the left, on an eminence, is a school founded in 1725 by John Wheelwright of North Shields for his tenants' children – more of the Wheelwright connection later. Drop down along the perimeter of Rishworth School, founded in 1724, and swing right to the A672.

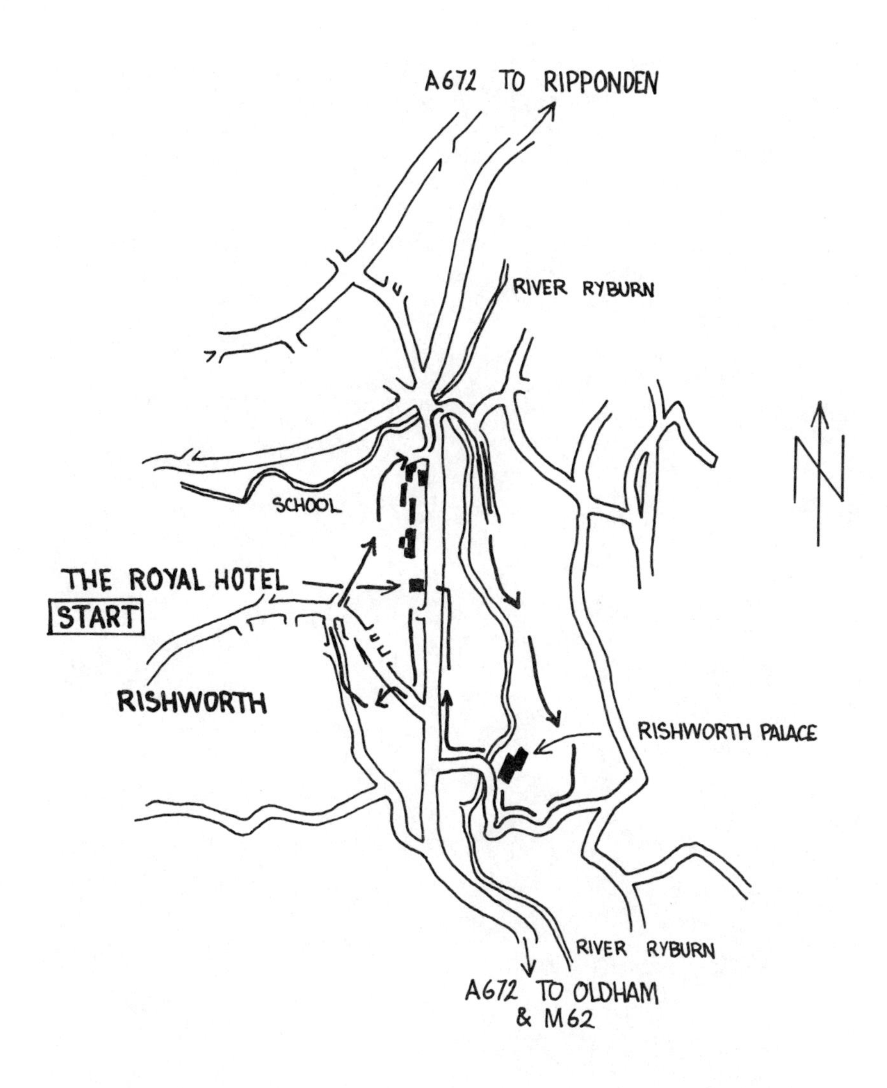

Turn left along the footway for 200 yards and, opposite lighting column 37, turn right, following the public footpath sign marked 'Holme House Lane'. Cross the river Ryburn on a bridge and turn right, following the bank and then ascending away from the river. Where the track swings sharp left, keep going forward to the left of the cottage (the route is not readily

A young map reader on the walk from Rishworth.

apparent) on a raised footpath. Go through a gap in a wall and enter a wood, then cross a stream on a bridge. There are attractive ferns along the margins here.

Keep going forward along the field edge to a stile. Cross this and keep streamside to the next stile, which you cross, aiming diagonally right for the barn. Turn right through the barn yard and swing left to the steps. Mount and go up the track to the gate. Go through and turn right past Mill House Farm. At the bend, examine the old sluice and the mill pond. Swing right to Rishworth Palace!

As many as 89 luxury apartments (complete with a fully equipped gymnasium and a laundrette) have been created in what was once one of the most productive cotton mills ever. Built by John Wheelwright's grandson, also named John, and opened in 1868, Rishworth New Mill housed one of the world's largest water wheels – it spanned almost 58 ft, was 12 ft broad and weighed 70 tons.

Continue over the bridge and turn right on the A672 footway, back to the inn.

Places of interest nearby

North of Rishworth is the old-world village of *Ripponden*, centred on a 650 year old inn and an arched packhorse bridge over the river Ryburn. See St Bartholomew's parish church and visit the *Ryburn Farm Museum* with its cottage kitchen, dairy, agricultural store and hand-loom weaving chamber. Near Ripponden, at *Blackstone Edge*, is a magnificently preserved portion of the Roman road between Manchester and Ilkley. Set 16 ft apart, deeply embedded stone kerbs retain a roadway consisting of a series of large slabs grooved in the middle – probably once filled with turves to assist the horses gain purchase up the steep hill.

17 Midgley
The Black Bull

The hamlet of Midgley occupies a lofty, green belt position midway between Barnsley, Huddersfield and Wakefield. The Black Bull, an elevated and accommodating beast whose expanded girth integrates a former barn, offers the most modern of welcomes. Crowned by original roof timbers, the five elegantly furnished, interconnecting rooms are decorated with old farming implements and prints.

The extensive standard menu features chicken escalopes with lemon, fillet of salmon, steak and mushroom pudding, marinated lamb steak, gammon and beef steaks, vegetable moussaka and a range of fresh salad platters and light bites. Children have their own menu. The daily specials board typically includes tagliatelle niçoise, spicy lamb pepperpot, jumbo cod and beef curry. Over 75% of the dining area is reserved for non smokers. The house ales are hand-pulled Whitbread Trophy and Boddingtons Bitter and a guest beer. The choices of lager are Heineken and Stella, and draught

Guinness is also available. A small patio is situated to the rear of the inn, which is increasingly popular with families.

The opening times are from 11 am to 11 pm on Monday to Saturday, and 12 noon to 3 pm and 7 pm to 10.30 pm on Sunday.

Telephone: 01924 830260.

How to get there: The inn is on the A637 east of Huddersfield and can be reached from junctions 38 and 39 of the M1.

Parking: There is adequate parking with overspill provision at the inn. 'Pay and display' facilities are available at the Sculpture Park.

Length of the walk: 1¼ miles. OS map: Landranger 110 (inn GR 273147).

Bretton Hall College, overlooking the lower lake.

The National Coal Mining Museum at Caphouse Colliery, Overton, near Wakefield.

In the interests of safety and ease, this walk is preceded by a short car ride to the unique Yorkshire Sculpture Park located in the grounds of Bretton Hall. Now a teacher training college, the Hall was once the home of Sir Thomas Wentworth who spectacularly landscaped the grounds towards the end of the 18th century. Two lakes support large numbers of birds and rare plants. Access to view the sculptures, which include works by former district residents Henry Moore and Barbara Hepworth, is free.

This relaxing and artistically stimulating saunter enjoys a grand landscape and the very best in modern sculpture, both in the open and in two indoor galleries.

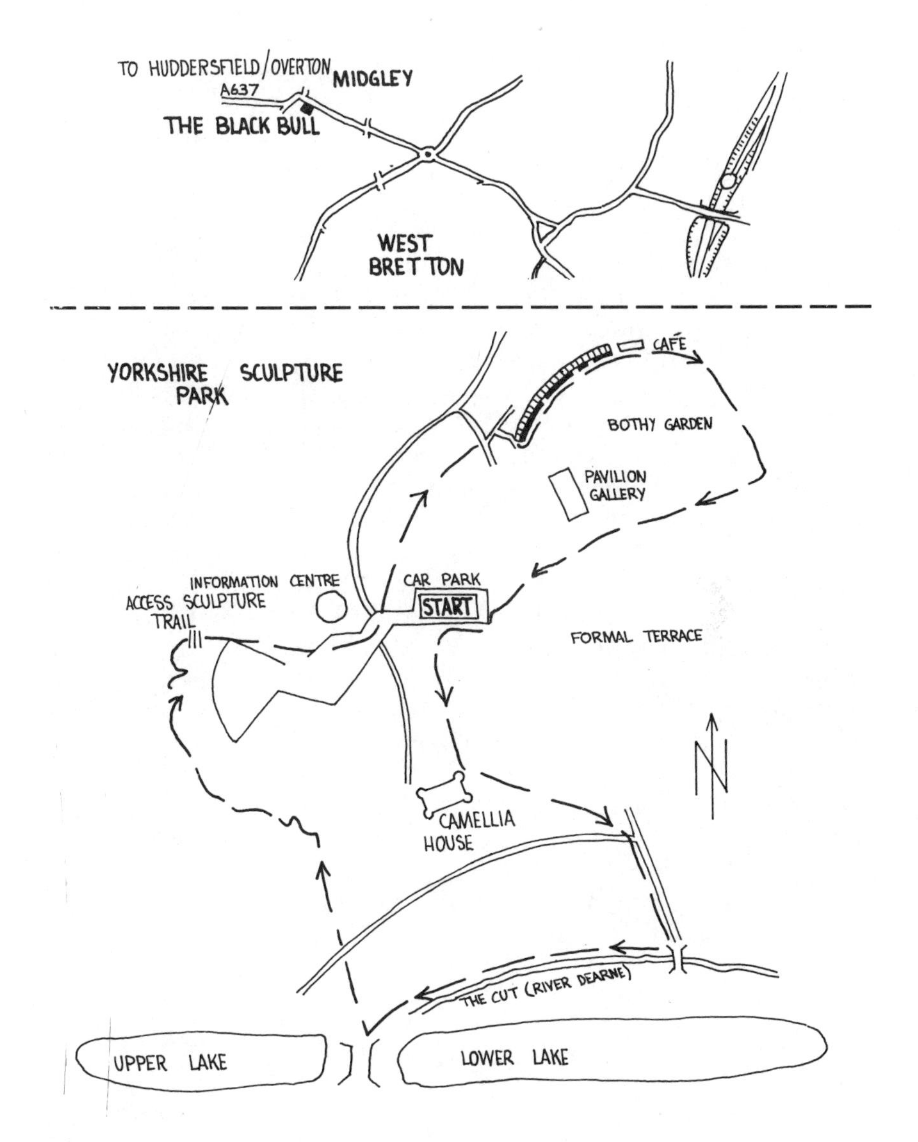

The Walk

Leave the pub car park and drive eastwards along the A637 for about 1 mile, following the signs for 'Barnsley/M1 South' and 'Yorkshire Sculpture Park'. Turn right in West Bretton, along Park Lane, following the park access sign and leave your car in the designated parking area.

From the information centre, follow the signs to the Bothy Café, uphill over the landscaped area, passing a number of highly original pieces. At the top of the hill, turn right and walk along the gravel path towards the gap in the conifer hedge. Swing left into what was the old kitchen garden and follow the wall up to the café, where lunches and light refreshments are available. You can also visit the Bothy Shop and Gallery and the Pavilion Gallery. Keep following the wall round, dropping down alongside the yew hedge to the corner. Go through a gap in the hedge and turn right along the Formal Terrace.

Walk back almost to the parking area and go left towards the Camellia House, swinging left downhill to the lakes and a green balustraded bridge over the cut (river Dearne). Access over the bridge into the nature reserves on both banks is restricted but permits are available from the College Finance Office. Turn right along the cut and, after about 250 yards, go over a stile and left onto a bridge to view the upper and lower lakes. Retrace your steps and recross the stile, going left across the playing fields, steering to the right of the fenced pond and continuing uphill. Aim for a point midway between the two central beech trees and go left, exploring the Access Sculpture Trail before swinging right, back to the car park.

Places of interest nearby

The National Mining Museum is just to the north-west, at Caphouse Colliery, Overton. Based at a redundant working mine, it offers descents to the coal face and a hands-on history of the industry that once dominated West Yorkshire.

18 Badsworth
The Rogerthorpe Manor Hotel

Crystal glassed and chandeliered, this Jacobean building is every bit the vision of manorial England. Set in aloof isolation, a tall gabled and ivied neighbour of one of the prettiest but least visited villages in Yorkshire – the destination for this walk – it is at once grand and welcoming, offering casual bar snacks as well as more sophisticated meals for formal diners.

Decorated in pastel shades and furnished with matching leather settees, the Taverners Bar offers a range of food, including sandwiches, smoked salmon with scrambled eggs, toasted baguette with garlic, lasagne al forno, gammon steak, steak and kidney pie and seasonal specialities of the day. The adjoining Oak Room restaurant, which is popular for Sunday lunches (it is advisable to book), has an extensive menu listing pan-fried chicken breast, steak and kidney pudding, baked cod and speciality dishes such as entrecôte steak, steamed halibut, sauté pheasant, potato pancakes and Chinese vegetable and nut stir-fry. The bar top line is John Smith's hand-pulled bitter,

Badsworth church.

Foster's lager and draught Beamish stout. For a longer stay, the hotel has twelve luxury bedrooms, as well as excellent conference and banquet facilities, and it is surrounded by beautiful gardens.

The bar opening times on Monday to Saturday are from 11 am to 11 pm. Sunday hours are from 12 noon to 3 pm and 7 pm to 10.30 pm.

Telephone: 01977 643839.

How to get there: The hotel is on the B6474 Thorpe Lane, between the villages of Thorpe Audlin and Badsworth and is 2½ miles south-west of the A1 at Wentbridge.

Parking: Ample parking is available.

Length of the walk: 1¾ miles. OS map: Landranger 111 (inn GR 479153).

Through fields to peaceful Badsworth village. Will you unravel an abiding mystery? Buried underfoot, so legend has it, are several stained glass windows, removed from St Mary's church during the Civil War to preserve them from being vandalised by the Parliamentarians. The churchyard is where you will linger most. The gravestones are leaves of a history book writ large.

The Walk

Leave the hotel grounds and cross the road, turning left along the footway. Continue for 150 yards and turn right, following the public bridleway sign, for about 600 yards. Go left on a farm trackway, walking towards farm buildings. Swing left in front of the farmhouse and continue on the track. Pass a house on the right – house sign 'Jelemy Tump' – and go left on Grove Lane.

Turn left on Ninevah Lane and left again on Main Street. Pass Badsworth Hall on the left (the original and more substantial building was demolished in 1940, leaving the former stable block to take on the mantle). Swing right and go left through the churchyard, following the public footpath sign. One of the most intriguing monuments in the churchyard is in the shape of a pyramid, raised to the memory of a native of Hindustan.

Swing left along the flagged causeway, leave the churchyard, passing to the left of the school, and continue through the

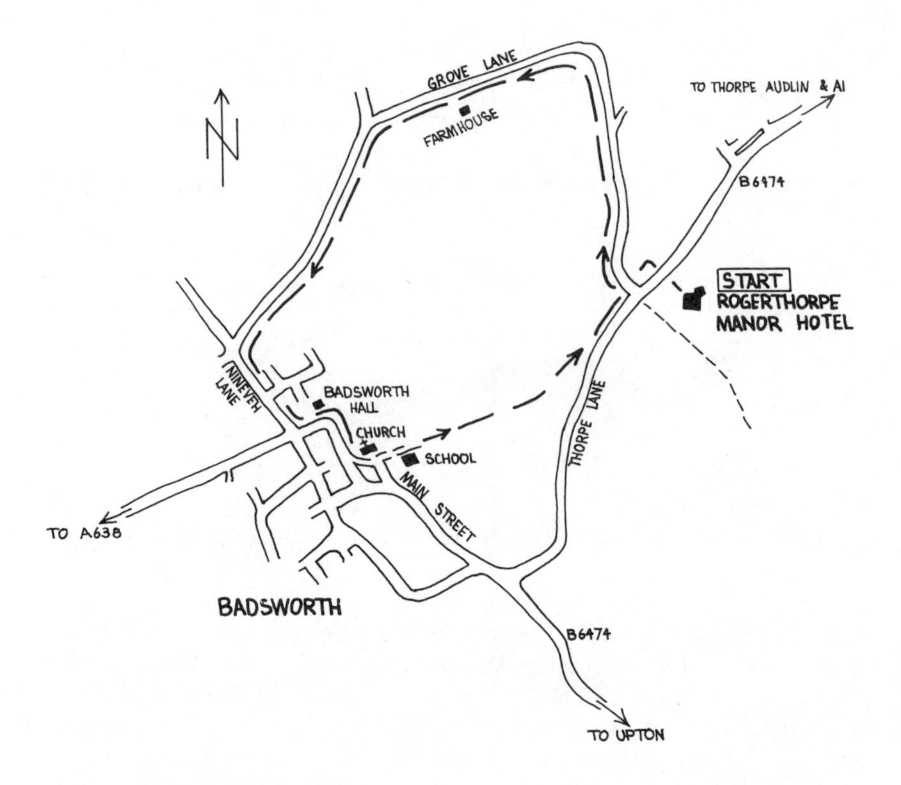

kissing-gate. Keep fenceside on the footpath and go through the next kissing-gate hedgeside to the final kissing-gate and the road. Turn left along the footway for 200 yards and turn right, back to the hotel.

Places of interest nearby

Some 6 miles to the north-west along the A638 is *Nostell Priory*, the 18th-century stately home of Lord St Oswald, designed by James Paine with interior decoration by Robert Adam. It houses a splendid collection of Chippendale furniture, including a unique dolls' house. The grounds include a craft centre, a picnic park, an adventure playground, lakeside walks and a rose garden.

19 Scissett
The Crown

This linear village extends for a mile along the wooded banks of the river Dearne. Textiles have fuelled the local economy for generations and lofty mills, some now converted for alternative uses, still dominate the scene. St Augustine's church, built in 1839 is one of the best roadside buildings. It has a particularly fine iron screen carved with flowers and scrolls. The winding lane south-east of the village leads to the 239 acre Deffer Wood – a beauty spot and nature reserve.

Behind a big and bold exterior, the thoroughly modernised Crown reveals a quality conversion geared for the new generation of pubgoers. The Victorian theme, employing brass, stained glass and pastel drapes, is co-ordinated throughout to create an attractive place for the whole family. The long front bar provides, at one end, a top-of-the-range pool table and a discreetly housed Big Screen TV, which miraculously pops up on match days!

The main catering area is the 40-seater facility to the rear.

Echoeing the multi-age/multi-attraction concept, the menu offers speciality steaks, traditional dishes such as steak and kidney pie and steak and mushroom suet pudding, and more cosmopolitan choices like tagliatelle carbonara and chicken tikka masala. Daily specials may include beef in ale pie, coq au vin and minty lamb. Children have their own low-priced menu. A wide range of beers, lagers and wines complements the food and includes hand-pulled Boddingtons and Trophy Bitter (plus guests), Murphy's stout, Guinness, and Heineken and Stella lagers. The pub is readily accessible to wheelchairs and there are separate purpose-built disabled toilet facilities.

The opening times are from 11 am to 11 pm on Monday to Saturday. Sunday hours are from 12 noon to 10.30 pm (alcoholic drinks are reserved for diners only between 3 pm and 7 pm).

Telephone: 01484 862358.

How to get there: The pub is in a prominent roadside position in the village of Scissett, on the A636 near Denby Dale.

Parking: There is a large car park.

Length of the walk: 2 miles. OS map: Landranger 110 (inn GR 247102).

Within a clog toss of the old mill yards, this ramble over scenic parts of the Kirklees Way takes you along wooded paths into the grounds of Bagden Hall – with a nostalgic whiff of steam at the end.

The Walk

Turn right from the pub along Wakefield Road and pass the 1839 church of St Augustine. Turn next right past Dearne Cottages and swing left, going next right along Lower Common Lane. Walk uphill for 150 yards and opposite the bungalow, Cranbrooke, turn left, following the yellow arrowhead marker, signposted 'Kirklees Way', between a fence and a wall. Cross a stile and veer left, keeping in the bottom and aiming for the hedge corner by the cricket ground. Keep left, heading towards the woods and looking out for yellow-tipped posts between two hawthorn trees.

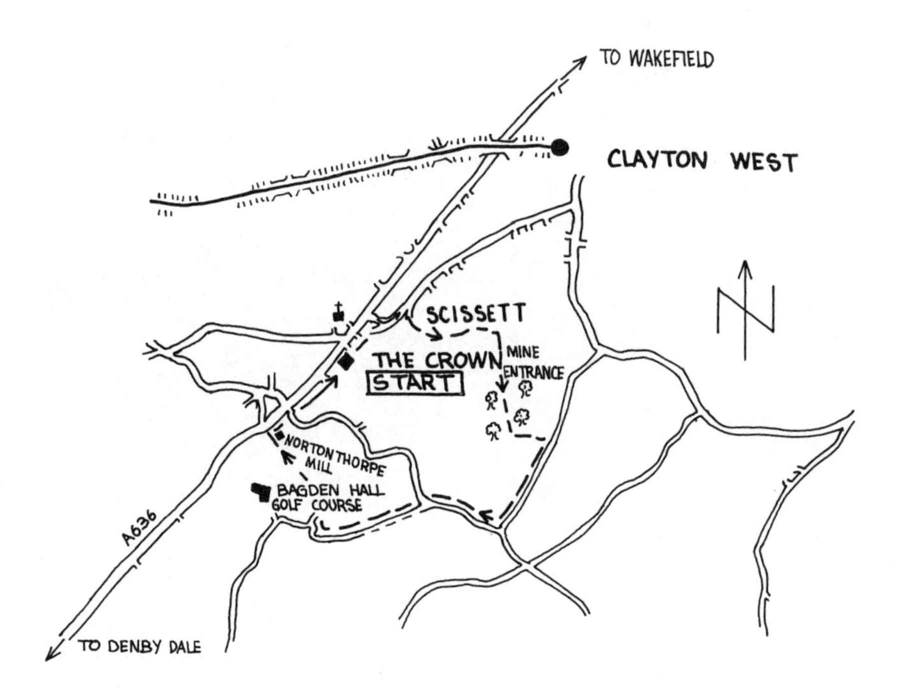

Go over a stile, following the 'Kirklees Way' marker along the field edge to the corner, then cross a stile into the woods, descending via steps. Cross a stream and weave right. At the next fork, keep right and pass an old, sinister mine entrance, swinging left. Veer right along a path, with a wall to the left, and drop down to the stream, going right across the stepping stones and left to a stile, which you cross.

Keep forward in the bottom and veer left across a field to find a public footpath sign and a kissing-gate in the wall on the roadside. Go through and turn right along the quiet road. Continue to the junction with Wheatley Hill Lane and turn right. Walk on, ignoring the first public footpath sign on the left, and go left at the next sign, along the track, passing the former gatehouse cottage. Pass the mine to the left, keeping straight ahead, then cross the stile by the gate and swing right over the bridge. Go right again, then left to a cottage. (Note the carved figures set into the wall.) Turn right through a kissing-gate and follow the directions and the white arrow markers across the

The Fox locomotive. (The Kirklees Light Railway Company Ltd)

golf course. This once was the private grounds of Bagden Hall, now a fashionable hotel and conference centre.

Leave the course and turn right for 10 yards, going diagonally left and following a public footpath sign through a gap in the wall, downhill. Go through the next kissing-gate and swing left, climbing wallside. Go left along Cuttlehurst, passing the interesting residential mill conversion of 1988 to the left and drop down to the old Nortonthorpe Mill complex. Here you will discover the charming Violet, a lovingly restored 1886 horizontal tandem, compound steam engine which for 76 years supplied all the mill's power. There are open days in April, August and November (other steam engines are also on display). For more details, telephone: 01484 863545 or 01924 444587. Passing the mill, continue to Wakefield Road and turn right, back to the pub.

Places of interest nearby

As well as being ideally placed for country walks, the pub is also convenient for the *Kirklees Light Railway*, just down the road in Clayton West. The 15 in gauge steam engines – appealing 0-6-4 saddle tank Badger and 2-6-2 side tank Fox – pull miniature carriages through the south Pennine foothills. A delight for youngsters. Open each weekend, and every day from Easter to mid-September (telephone: 01484 865727).

20 Upperthong
The Royal Oak

Although not very far from the 'Last of the Summer Wine' tourist haunts, Upperthong casts a snook at congested Holmfirth far below. The many visitors on the trail of Nora Batty's legendary wrinkled stockings somehow never get this far and Town Gate, with its old weavers' cottages and a delectable little acorn of a pub, is left in peace.

A pub since 1897, the Royal Oak is very much the centre of village life. Small but handsome, preserving outside its walls a venerable pump, and beyond its rugged portal (they don't make doors like this any more) traditional beams and fireplaces, it offers an inviting, one-roomed gem decorated with rustic prints. The rear beer garden has wonderful views. Home-made soups and loin-girding ham and eggs top the blackboard menu, which is influenced by the seasons but might include, for example, such dishes as cauliflower and leek in blue cheese, goujons of chicken and reef and beef. The Oak specialises in standard evening dinners – Monday is steak night, followed by chicken on Wednesday, fish on Friday and T-bones on Saturday. Children are welcome here for meals. The house ales are hand-pulled Worthington and Stones Bitter. Caffrey's Irish Ale and guests. Bass mild is also available, together with Tennent's and Carlsberg lagers and Guinness.

The opening times on Monday to Friday are from 12 noon to 3 pm and 5.30 pm to 11 pm. Weekend hours are 12 noon to 3 pm and 6 pm (7 pm on Sunday) to 11 pm.

Telephone: 01484 683450.

How to get there: There is easy but constricted access from Holmfirth, south of Huddersfield. Going west from the town centre, fork first right up the steep hill, keep going right, still ascending into Upperthong.

Parking: Only limited parking is available at the pub. Alternative parking can be found on-street or on the outskirts of the village.

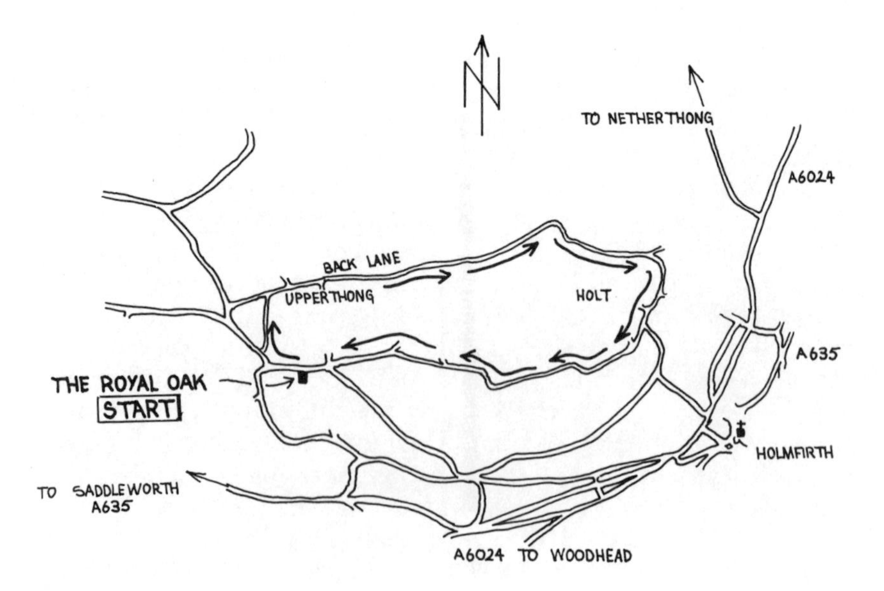

Length of the walk: 2 miles. OS map: Landranger 110 (inn GR 126085).

On this gentle hillsides ramble, along old, walled trackways, you may well encounter Compo, Foggy and Clegg – but beware the clapper boards.

The Walk

Turn left from the pub along Town Gate and turn right on Wickens Lane. After 50 yards go right, following the yellow arrow marker, over a stile along a track, wallside, towards woodland. Climb a wall via steps and cross a meadow to a gap in a wall. Go through and turn right along a track known as Back Lane.

Keep going forward along the walled track and gradually drop down towards a stream on the left. Swing right, away from the stream, and go right and left before swinging sharp right, walking on past the radio tower to the three-directional path

'Last of the Summer Wine' country – the moors south of Holmfirth.

sign. Keep going forward, passing the Holt and going along Hill, and swing right and left, merging with a walled track. Continue along the track back to Upperthong. Merge with Hill Lane and continue straight ahead along Town Gate back to the pub.

Places of interest nearby

As well as familiar scenes from your television screen, *Holmfirth* offers a fascinating postcard museum. The town should have beaten Hollywood to international acclaim. Here in the 1890s, the Bamforth Brothers experimented with early films.